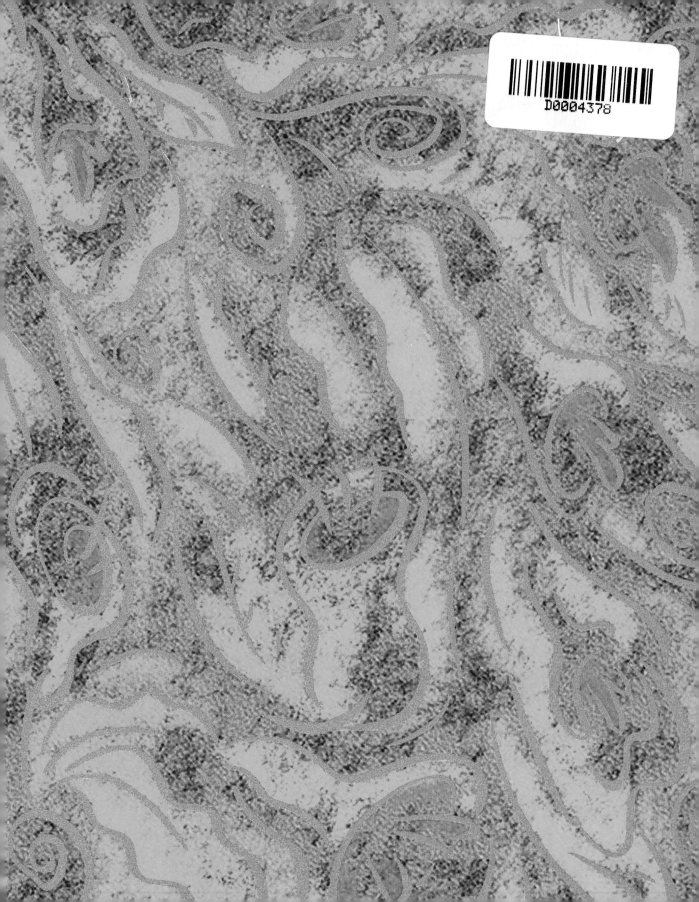

ITALY

THE BEAUTIFUL
COOKBOOK

One hundred best recipes by
LORENZA DE' MEDICI

Text by
PATRIZIA PASSIGLI

CollinsPublishersSanFrancisco
A Division of HarperCollins*Publishers*

Published in the U.S.A. in 1994 by
Collins Publishers San Francisco
1160 Battery Street San Francisco, CA 94111 USA

Conceived and produced by Weldon Owen Inc.
814 Montgomery Street San Francisco, CA 94133 USA

President: John Owen
Publisher: Jane Fraser
Project Editor: Ruth Jacobson
Editor: Janet Mowery
Editorial Assistant: Kim Green
Index: Ken DellaPenta
Design and Art Direction: John Bull
Design Layout: Ruth Jacobson
Color Illustration: Nicole Kaufman
Production: James Obata, Stephanie Sherman
Food Photography: Mike Hallson Photography
Food Styling: Jacki Passmore

ISBN 0-00-255464-X

The Beautiful Cookbook® series is a
registered trademark of Weldon Owen Inc.

Production by Mandarin Offset, Hong Kong
Printed in Hong Kong

Above: Ceramic tiles illustrating some of the many delights of Italian cuisine decorate a wall in Poppi.
Pages 4–5: The late afternoon sun basks the Ponte Santa Trinita in Florence with a golden light.
Pages 8–9: An abandoned farmhouse near Bagno Vignoni seems to blend into the surrounding countryside.
Even in the most remote areas of Italy lie subtle reminders of human presence on the land.

Photographs by Michael Freeman: pages 2, 4–5, 8–9
Photographs by Gian Luigi Scarfiotti: pages 6, 10, 14–15, 34, 48, 50, 62, 83, 97, 106, 109
Photograph by Fabbri Editori Milano: page 20

CONTENTS

INTRODUCTION

AN ITALIAN PROVERB SAYS, "At the table no one grows old." Perhaps this is why the taste for good food goes a long way back in time, as we know from a host of artistic, literary and scientific evidence.

The ancient Romans feasted on breads—often in the form of flat loaves *(focacce)*—legumes, cabbage, lettuce, figs, pears, plums and grapes. As Rome's conquests carried Latin customs beyond her borders, so too the Roman lifestyle was enriched with bounty from other lands. Gastronomy reached a peak of sophistication bordering on the dissolute. The famous supper of Trimalchio described by Petronius in his *Satyricon* (first century A.D.) paints a vivid picture:

"First of all we were offered a pie with a crown of sausages . . . and homemade bran bread. . . . The next dish was a cold cake with hot honey, over which Spanish wine had been poured. . . . After that we found before us a portion of bear meat. . . . And lastly we were offered soft cheese, fruit mustard, a snail for each person, some tripe, a dish of liver, some smothered eggs, turnips, mustard. . . . Then a bowl of olives in vinegar was passed around. . . . When the prosciutto arrived, we surrendered."

The art of cooking with all its refinements was not only for the wealthy. And so at the time of the Empire a number of works were dedicated to gastronomy as a science. There were guidebooks to the good life, with recipes and advice about health and the maintenance of house and garden.

In the Middle Ages an international cuisine began to take shape. In the kitchens of the courts and the aristocracy foods were flavored with spices from all over the world. During the fifteenth and sixteenth centuries, Italy led the rest of the world in the art of cooking, introducing formality in the form of recipes, table manners, and rules of presentation—ideas that Catherine de' Medici carried with her when she married the King of France.

Each era has its place in the development of the Italian culinary tradition. Perhaps none is more important, though, than the nineteenth century, when the so-called Russian serving style, with one course following another became the rule. The invention of a machine for making commercially produced pasta also goes back to the first decade of the nineteenth century. And in the 1840s the distinguishing bouquets of the major Italian wines were established, and Parmesan cheese took on its definitive form and flavor. The day of the costly and complicated "court cuisine" was finally over, and a new gastronomic culture was developing, in perfect accord with the middle-class lifestyle that was by this time triumphant all over Europe.

STUFFED PIGEONS (LEFT, RECIPE PAGE 76), BREAD SALAD WITH TOMATO (TOP RIGHT, RECIPE PAGE 42) AND TUSCAN RICE (BOTTOM RIGHT, RECIPE PAGE 30), PHOTOGRAPHED AT BADIA A COLTIBUONO, THE AUTHOR'S RESIDENCE.

GLI ANTIPASTI

A N ANTIPASTO comes before the meal *(il pasto)*, and its function is to prepare the stomach for the courses to follow, by stimulating the production of gastric juices. So the *antipasto* is to be merely tasted, savored slowly in minimal amounts rather than devoured. Otherwise it takes the place of the meal, becoming an epilogue instead of a prologue.

Italian *antipasti* follow one general rule: hot ones are served before a reasonably light meal, cold ones before a substantial meal. Both hot and cold are commonly served at cocktail parties and receptions. Also, they must have a certain harmony with the rest of the menu—they should bear some relation to the dishes that follow.

The visual element of *antipasti* dishes is important, so that the appetite is stimulated in the imagination even before it is stimulated by the taste. A skillful blending of colors and garnishes is all part of the exercise: preparing a plate of *antipasti* is like playing with a puzzle.

Another factor to be considered is that *antipasti* often include raw vegetables; to keep them from darkening once they have been cut, one must use a very sharp stainless steel knife and keep the vegetables covered until they are served.

Although they are drawn from many different areas, most of these recipes have decidely "poor" origins, as the ingredients clearly show: eggplant, anchovies, tomatoes, *focaccia*. And most of the recipes here have one indispensable ingredient in common: extra virgin olive oil. Just as olive trees have been a constant feature of the Italian landscape for thousands of years, so olive oil has always played a leading role in Italian cooking—at least in three-quarters of the peninsula. There is an old saying that wine lifts the spirits and oil lifts the taste, which explains the dominant role of olive oil in the kitchens of peasant and aristocrat alike. The Roman *bruschetta,* the Piedmontese *carpaccio,* seafood salads, the Tuscan raw vegetable dip *pinzimonio*—none would be the same without the unmistakable taste of extra virgin olive oil.

The only one of these recipes that requires any elaborate preparation, in comparison with the simplicity of the others, is the eggplant with mozzarella, which needs to be cooked in two stages. This dish was originally created as a complete one-course meal for the tables of Sicilian peasant farmers; it contained a perfect balance of vitamins, proteins and fats in the form of vegetables, cheese and olive oil.

PARMESAN CARPACCIO (LEFT, RECIPE PAGE 17) AND
PEPPERS WITH ANCHOVIES (RIGHT, RECIPE PAGE 17)

11

EGGPLANT WITH MOZZARELLA

Campania

MELANZANE ALLA MOZZARELLA
EGGPLANT WITH MOZZARELLA

Eggplant is one of the most popular vegetables in the cooking of Campania. It is fried, grilled, sautéed in slices with a little oil, or used to add flavor to pizzas and spaghetti. Best for cooking are the very dark purple, long eggplants, which have few seeds. Firmness to the touch and a shiny skin indicate freshness.

12 slices eggplant (aubergine), cut ⅜ in
   (1 cm) thick
salt

12 tomato slices
12 fresh basil leaves
12 thin slices mozzarella
¼ cup (2 fl oz/60 ml) extra virgin olive oil
freshly ground pepper

Lightly sprinkle the eggplant slices with salt on both sides. Place them between two plates and top with a weight. Let eggplant drain for about an hour.

Salt the tomato slices and let them drain for 1 hour.

Pat the eggplant slices dry. Cook them on a hot grill for a few minutes on each side or until tender. Arrange them on a plate and place a tomato slice, a mozzarella slice and a basil leaf on each. Drizzle with oil, season with salt and pepper and serve.

Serves 6

Toscana

CROSTINI DI FEGATINI
CHICKEN LIVER CROUTONS

Chicken liver croutons are a classical component of Tuscan antipasto dishes and usually accompany prosciutto, salami and finocchiona *(a sausage strongly flavored with fennel seeds). In recent years the croutons have also become popular garnished with chopped tomato and flavored with basil and extra virgin olive oil.*

1–2 *porcini* mushrooms or champignons
extra virgin olive oil
4 large chicken livers
6 fresh sage leaves
2 garlic cloves, chopped
freshly ground pepper
½ cup (4 fl oz/125 ml) *vin santo*★
salt
1 anchovy fillet
1 heaping tablespoon capers, drained
1 egg yolk (see glossary)
milk, if needed
12 slices firm, coarse-textured bread

🔥 Soak the mushrooms in hot water and cover for at least 10 minutes. Drain well.
🔥 Heat 2 tablespoons olive oil in a heavy-bottomed skillet over medium-high heat. Add the chicken livers, sage, garlic, mushrooms and some pepper and cook, stirring constantly, for about 10 minutes or until the livers have lost their red color. Add the *vin santo* and cook until evaporated. Season with salt to taste.

🔥 Add the anchovy fillet and capers. Transfer mixture to food processor and purée. Blend in the egg yolk.

🔥 Preheat an oven to 375°F (190°C). Lightly coat the slices of bread on both sides with olive oil and toast in the oven until golden brown. Allow to cool. Spread the mixture on the croutons and serve immediately.

★Vin santo *is a Tuscan dessert wine. Substitute a dessert wine or sweet Marsala.*

Serves 6

CHICKEN LIVER CROUTONS

SCHIACCIATA AL ROSMARINO
FLAT BREAD WITH ROSEMARY

Tuscan schiacciata, *a flat pizza-type bread, is usually sprinkled only with oil and coarse salt, but it can also be flavored with rosemary or sage. It is similar to the Ligurian* focaccia, *which has thinly sliced onions or olives scattered on it.*

½ oz (15 g) fresh yeast or 1 envelope
 (¼ oz/7 g) dry yeast
½ cup (4 fl oz/125 ml) tepid water
4 cups (20 oz/620 g) bread flour or
 all–purpose (plain) flour
3 tablespoons extra virgin olive oil
leaves of 1 large fresh rosemary sprig
coarse salt

Dissolve the yeast in tepid water and let stand for 10 minutes. Heap the flour on a board and make a well in the center. Pour the dissolved yeast into this and add sufficient water to make a soft dough. Knead the dough until smooth and elastic, at least 10 minutes. Form it into a ball. Sprinkle the inside of a large bowl with flour. Place dough in bowl and cover with a clean cloth. Let stand in a warm place until doubled in volume.

Knead the dough again briefly. Roll out on a lightly floured baking sheet into a circle about ⅜ in (1 cm) thick. Let rise again for 30 minutes. Brush the top with oil and sprinkle with rosemary and coarse salt. Bake in a preheated 450°F (230°C) oven until golden brown. Let cool slightly before serving.

Serves 6

FLAT BREAD WITH ROSEMARY (TOP) AND
GARLIC TOAST (BOTTOM, RECIPE PAGE 16)

HAM AND MELON

Emilia - Romagna

PROSCIUTTO E MELONE
HAM AND MELON

This is certainly one of the best-known Italian summer hors d'oeuvres. The ham produced in San Daniele, in the Friuli region, is considered to be the best, but the most famous without doubt is that of Parma. In Tuscany the ham is saltier; sometimes it is made from wild boar, in which case it is very lean and full of flavor. This prosciutto (uncooked ham) can also be served with figs or kiwi fruit.

1 large ripe cantaloupe (rockmelon) or
   honeydew melon
freshly ground pepper
12 slices prosciutto

Peel the melon and cut into slivers, removing seeds and fibers. Arrange the slivers radiating out from the center of a serving plate. Sprinkle with pepper.

Lightly curl the slices of ham and drape one over each melon slice. Chill well and serve.

Serves 6

Lazio

BRUSCHETTA
GARLIC TOAST

In Rome it is called bruschetta, *in Tuscany* fett'unta *(literally "oiled slice"): the important thing is that this should be made with bread that has excellent taste and texture, and with a good-quality extra virgin olive oil.* Bruschetta *can also be served with slices of tomato and a few fresh basil leaves. Sometimes the tomato is rubbed into the bread with the garlic.*

6 slices coarse-textured bread, cut ⅜ in
   (1 cm) thick
3 garlic cloves, halved
6 tablespoons (3 fl oz/90 ml) extra virgin
   olive oil
salt and freshly ground pepper

Toast the bread slices, and while still hot rub each well with the cut side of a garlic clove. Drizzle a tablespoon of olive oil over each slice. Add a little salt and plenty of pepper. Serve immediately.

Serves 6   *Photograph pages 14–15*

PEPERONI ALLE ACCIUGHE
PEPPERS WITH ANCHOVIES

This is one of the classic antipasto *dishes of Piedmont. The peppers that grow around Asti are highly prized for their plumpness and sweet taste. They are also eaten raw, cut into strips and dipped in* bagna cauda, *a hot, garlic-flavored anchovy dip.*

4 anchovy fillets preserved in salt
3 bell peppers (capsicums), a combination of
   yellow (or green) and red
1 tablespoon finely chopped fresh oregano
1 garlic clove, very thinly sliced
1 tablespoon capers, drained and finely
   chopped
salt
¼ cup (2 fl oz/60 ml) extra virgin olive oil

Wash anchovy fillets under running water for several minutes to rid them of their salt. Bone them and cut into small pieces. Wash, dry and halve the peppers; remove ribs and seeds. Bake in a preheated 400°F (200°C) oven for 20 minutes. Remove from oven and let cool. Cut into strips.

Place peppers on a serving dish and sprinkle with oregano, garlic, capers and anchovies. Season with salt to taste. Drizzle with oil.

Let stand for 2 hours to blend flavors before serving.

Serves 12   *Photograph page 10*

CARNE CRUDA ALLA PARMIGIANA
PARMESAN CARPACCIO

Carpaccio, *the famous dish launched by Arrigo Cipriani at Harry's Bar in Venice, has in reality always been the main component of the delicious* Piedmontese *antipasto assortment. Traditionally, these wafer-thin slices of raw meat are garnished with flakes of Parmesan cheese, finely sliced white truffle, olive oil, lemon juice and salt.*

1 egg, hard-boiled (hard-cooked)
2 oz (60 g) Parmesan cheese (in one piece)
½ celery stalk, including leaves
8 oz (250 g) rump roast (steak), sliced
   paper thin
2 tablespoons fresh lemon juice
salt and freshly ground pepper
¼ cup (2 fl oz/60 ml) extra virgin olive oil
1 tablespoon very fine julienne strips of
   lemon peel

Sieve the hard-cooked egg. Shave very thin slices from the Parmesan cheese.

Mince the celery and the celery leaves separately.

Lay the meat slices on a serving plate and sprinkle with lemon juice, salt, pepper and oil.

Cover meat with cheese, minced celery and leaves, lemon peel and sieved egg. Serve immediately.

Serves 6   *Photograph page 10*

LITTLE PIZZAS

PIZZELLE

LITTLE PIZZAS

These little pizzas are often served as part of family meals in Neapolitan homes. They are traditionally topped with tomato and Parmesan cheese but are also very good with ricotta, or with endive sautéed in oil and garlic. A similar dish is served in Emilia-Romagna, where it is called gnocchi fritti *or "fried gnocchi."*

1 cup (5 oz/155 g) bread flour or all-purpose (plain) flour
¼ teaspoon dry yeast
5 tablespoons lukewarm water
1 lb (500 g) ripe tomatoes, peeled and coarsely chopped
salt
1 tablespoon sugar
4 garlic cloves
1 red chili pepper
3 tablespoons extra virgin olive oil
3 cups (24 fl oz/750 ml) oil for deep frying
6 fresh basil leaves

☙ Place the flour in a large bowl. Dissolve the yeast in 1 tablespoon lukewarm water and add to flour. Gradually add the remaining water to the flour, mixing until a firm, elastic dough forms. Knead for a few minutes. Form into a ball and let rise in a warm place for about 2 hours.

☙ To prepare the sauce: place tomatoes in a saucepan with a little salt and the sugar. Cook over medium heat until they are softened and the liquid has evaporated. Chop the garlic with the chili pepper. Sauté them in the olive oil until garlic is lightly colored. Stir into the tomato sauce and keep hot.

Roll the dough into a log 1 in (2.5 cm) thick. Cut into 1-inch (2.5-cm) pieces. Roll out each piece on a floured work surface.

Heat the oil in a cast iron skillet and fry the pizzas, turning once, until puffy and light brown.

Drain pizzas on paper towels and transfer to a serving platter. Add the basil to the tomato sauce. Serve sauce with the pizzas. Garnish with basil leaves.

Serves 4

Lombardia

INSALATA DI PETTI DI POLLO
CHICKEN SALAD WITH WALNUTS

This famous old recipe from Mantua once stipulated breast of capon rather than chicken breast, because it is more tender. In many regions of Italy capons are bred solely for the traditional Christmas dinner and are served boiled with green sauce or mostarda di Cremona, *which is a fruit relish consisting of candied fruit preserved in a spicy mustard syrup.*

1 carrot, chopped
1 green celery stalk, chopped
a handful of parsley (½ cup loosely packed)
1 bay leaf
2 cups (16 fl oz/500 ml) water
salt
1 whole chicken breast, about 8 oz (250 g)
2 tablespoons raisins
1 inner white celery stalk, cut into fine
   julienne strips

1 tablespoon fresh lemon juice
3 tablespoons extra virgin olive oil
1 small head of lettuce, divided into leaves
8 walnuts, shelled and chopped
chopped parsley (optional)

Combine the carrot, green celery, parsley, bay leaf and water in a saucepan. Add salt to taste. Bring to boil and simmer, partially covered, for about 30 minutes.

Add the chicken breast and poach just until firm and cooked through. Drain, cool, then skin and cut into julienne strips.

Soak raisins in lukewarm water for about 30 minutes; drain. Mix celery strips, chicken and drained raisins.

Whisk the lemon juice, oil and a pinch of salt. Arrange the lettuce in 6 small bowls or on a serving plate. Spoon the chicken salad into each lettuce leaf. Drizzle with the oil and lemon dressing. Decorate with walnuts or parsley and serve.

Serves 6

CHICKEN SALAD WITH WALNUTS

I PRIMI

PASTA IS UNDENIABLY *the* great factor in the Italian diet. It is an extraordinary invention that has become a trademark of Italian culture, and it is a food that has remained constant through the centuries.

Pasta, as the name clearly indicates (the Italian word *pasta* also means pastry or dough), is a "paste" made from flour (wheat, buckwheat, etc.), water and salt. With eggs added, it becomes "Sunday pasta." The first pasta-making machines were invented just over a hundred years ago; before that it was made by hand, mainly in the kitchens of southern Italian homes. This skill belonged to the female members of the family and was passed from mother to daughter. Its spread throughout the world was due not only to those early Italian women but also to the cooks in Italian courts of the late sixteenth century, who began to export this gastronomical wonder abroad. It is said that when Catherine de' Medici became the bride of the King of France, she took with her the recipe for a famous pasta pie, *Maccheroni alla Medici,* which included among its ingredients thrushes, truffles and a sauce of mushrooms.

Today, Italian *bucatini, maccheroni, tagliatelle, lasagne, rigatoni, fusilli, orecchiette, vermicelli, farfalle, torciglioni* and spaghetti, produced by the 240 pasta factories throughout the country, travel the world bringing in over 1,650 billion *lire* annually.

After pasta, Italians love rice. The Venetians' "national dish" of rice and peas was even served at ceremonial banquets in the dining halls of the Doge. Rice became firmly established in the north during the seventeenth century, while in the south macaroni and spaghetti were dominant.

Rice is an energy-giving food, light and very nutritious. There are various types, known as common, semifine, fine and superfine according to the length of the grain. The common variety is preferred for soups; the semifine for *antipasto* dishes, buttered rice, *supplì* and molded rice dishes; and the fine or superfine for *risotto* and side dishes.

The oldest kinds of first course, with their origins lost in antiquity are those based on bread, such as *canederli,* bread soups like *acquacotta, ribollita,* and *pappa al pomodoro; panzanella, pancotto, passatelli . . .* and the fourteenth-century *panunto* and *panlavato.* Gnocchi were also made with leftover bread.

The success of these dishes depends largely on the quality of the bread, which nowadays, at least in major cities, no longer has the consistency it once had. When soaked, instead of crumbling it becomes a glutinous mass that is unsuitable for the bread-based soups mentioned above. But with patience and perseverance it is still possible, particularly in country areas, to find real high-quality bread.

POTATO GNOCCHI (RECIPE PAGE 46)

21

Friuli-Venezia Giulia

IOTA
VEGETABLE SOUP OF TRIESTE

Iota is a soup of white beans, cabbage and bacon fat that shows the Austrian influence. It is a typical dish of Trieste, and for special occasions it is sometimes enriched with pieces of pork. Very simple and tasty, iota is a classic dish in the homes of the poor, as polenta once was in the Veneto.

1½ cups (10 oz/315 g) dried white beans
3 oz (90 g) bacon fat or salt pork, chopped
2 bay leaves
8 cups (64 fl oz/2 l) water
¼ cup (2 fl oz/60 ml) extra virgin olive oil
2 garlic cloves, crushed
1 tablespoon all-purpose (plain) flour
1 lb (500 g) cabbage, chopped
⅔ cup (3 oz/90 g) cornmeal
salt and freshly ground pepper

Soak the beans in cold water to cover for 12 hours. Drain and place in a saucepan with bacon fat and bay leaves. Add the water and simmer for 1 hour.

Heat oil in a deep skillet. Add garlic and flour and fry until golden. Add the cabbage and cook over very low heat for 5 minutes. Add this mixture to the beans and cook for 5 minutes. Sprinkle in cornmeal and mix well.

Season with salt and pepper and simmer for 45 minutes. Pour the soup into bowls and serve.

Serves 6–8

Trentino-Alto Adige

MINESTRA D'ORZO
BARLEY SOUP

In the Trentino region barley often replaces beans in soup. It can be cooked with vegetables such as cabbage or peas and is particularly good if a ham bone, boiled pork rind or small pork ribs are added to the stock and removed at the end of cooking.

1 cup (7 oz/220 g) pearl barley
2 tablespoons unsalted butter
3 oz (90 g) *pancetta* or rindless bacon, chopped
½ onion, chopped
1 celery stalk, chopped
1 shallot, chopped
8 cups (64 fl oz/2 l) broth (stock)
1 tablespoon chopped parsley

Soak the barley in cold water to cover for 12 hours. Drain. Melt butter in a large skillet and sauté the bacon, onion, celery and shallot until onion is translucent. Pour in the broth and bring to boil. Add the barley and cook until tender, about 1 hour.

Pour the soup into a tureen, sprinkle with parsley and serve.

Serves 6

VEGETABLE SOUP OF TRIESTE (TOP)
AND BARLEY SOUP (BOTTOM)

CHICKPEA SOUP

Lazio

MINESTRA DI CECI

CHICKPEA SOUP

Dried legumes such as chickpeas, beans and lentils are often the basis of tasty soups, either thick or thin, particularly in winter when fresh vegetables are more difficult to come by. In soups, short pasta is used; it may be thick or thin, but it always has a hole in the middle.

10 oz (310 g) dried chickpeas (garbanzo beans)
8 cups (64 fl oz/2 l) broth (stock)
1 fresh rosemary sprig
6 tablespoons (3 fl oz/90 ml) extra virgin
    olive oil
2 garlic cloves, chopped
1 can (8 oz/250 g) peeled tomatoes
1 cup (4 oz/125 g) *cannolicchi* pasta
salt and freshly ground pepper

Wash the chickpeas well and soak them in cold water to cover for 12 hours. Drain chickpeas and place in a saucepan with the broth and rosemary. Bring slowly to boil, then simmer for 2 hours.

Put half the chickpeas through a sieve with their cooking liquid or purée in a food processor. Heat the oil in a saucepan over moderate heat. Add the garlic and fry gently until the garlic colors. Add the tomatoes and cook for about 10 minutes to blend the flavors. Add the whole and puréed chickpeas with broth and bring to boil, then immediately add the pasta and cook until *al dente,* about 4–5 minutes. Taste for salt and pepper and serve immediately. Garnish with rosemary.

Serves 6

STRACCIATELLA
ROMAN EGG SOUP

Stracciatella *is a classic Roman soup with a very delicate taste. These days it is also found in the cooking of many other areas of Italy, especially Bologna. The breadcrumbs may be replaced by the same quantity of semolina, and a little grated nutmeg or parsley may be added.*

3 cups (24 fl oz/750 ml) chicken broth (stock)
3 eggs
¼ cup (½ oz/15 g) fresh breadcrumbs
¼ cup (1 oz/30 g) freshly grated Parmesan cheese
salt and freshly ground pepper
chopped parsley

❧ Bring the broth to boil in a saucepan. In a bowl, beat together the eggs, breadcrumbs and cheese. Add salt and pepper to taste.

❧ Remove broth from heat and pour in the egg mixture, blending well with a whisk. Return broth to a boil, stirring constantly with a whisk.

❧ Pour soup into small bowls, sprinkle with parsley and serve.

Serves 6

ROMAN EGG SOUP (LEFT) AND SOUP OF THE VAL D'AOSTA (RIGHT, RECIPE PAGE 27)

Lombardia

ZUPPA PAVESE
PAVIA SOUP

Pavia is a small and very old city to the south of Milan, and this soup is its specialty. The type of broth used is very important to the success of the dish: it must be clear broth made from fairly lean meat or from chicken, which can then be used to make a salad.

3 tablespoons unsalted butter
6 slices firm, coarse-textured bread
6 cups (48 fl oz/1.5 l) meat or chicken
   broth (stock)
salt
6 eggs
freshly ground pepper
⅓ cup (1½ oz/40 g) freshly grated Parmesan
   cheese
chopped parsley (optional)
grated nutmeg (optional)

🍲 Melt the butter in a saucepan and fry the bread slices on both sides until golden brown. Divide among 6 soup bowls. Place bowls in an oven which has been preheated to 350°F (180°C) and turned off.

🍲 Meanwhile, bring broth to boil, adding salt if necessary. Break an egg onto each slice of bread, pour the boiling broth over it and add pepper to taste. Sprinkle with Parmesan. Garnish with chopped parsley and a little grated nutmeg if desired and serve.

Serves 6

PAVIA SOUP

Val d'Aosta

ZUPPA VALDOSTANA
SOUP OF THE VAL D'AOSTA

The Val d'Aosta is a region surrounded by some of the highest mountains in Italy, including Mont Blanc. Its soups are rich and its flavors strong, to suit the bracing climate and the skiers who flock to the area's snow runs.

1¾ lb (875 g) cabbage
8 cups (64 fl oz/2 l) meat broth (stock)
2 tablespoons unsalted butter
6 slices firm, coarse-textured bread
7 oz (220 g) fontina or Gruyère cheese,
   very thinly sliced
freshly ground pepper

🍲 Remove the tough ribs from the cabbage. Drop cabbage into a pan of boiling water and blanch for 5 minutes. Slice cabbage, combine in a saucepan with the broth and simmer for 1 hour.

🍲 Melt butter in a skillet, add bread and fry until golden. Arrange bread slices in an earthenware baking dish and cover with half the cheese slices. Sprinkle with pepper. Pour in the broth and cabbage, cover with remaining cheese and finish cooking in a preheated 325°F (160°C) oven for 30 minutes before serving.

Serves 6   *Photograph page 25*

VEGETABLE SOUP WITH RICE

Lombardia

MINESTRONE DI RISO
VEGETABLE SOUP WITH RICE

In Lombardy a thick minestrone with rice is most often eaten in summer, served cold. The rice is only minimally cooked, as it continues to cook when poured into the soup bowls. If the soup is to be served hot, the rice is cooked for 16 minutes and the minestrone is then served immediately.

1 cup (6 oz/185 g) dried *borlotti* (pinto/ red kidney) beans

2 oz (60 g) *pancetta* or rindless bacon, finely chopped
1 onion, finely chopped
2 tablespoons unsalted butter
2 celery stalks, diced
2 carrots, diced
2 zucchini (courgettes), diced
2 boiling potatoes, diced
salt and freshly ground pepper
4 large ripe tomatoes, peeled and chopped
1 tablespoon tomato paste (purée)
8 cups (64 fl oz/2 l) meat broth (stock)
1 cup (5 oz/155 g) green beans, cut into short lengths
½ cup (3 oz/90 g) Arborio rice
6 tablespoons freshly grated Parmesan cheese
2 tablespoons chopped parsley

❧ Soak *borlotti* beans overnight in cold water to cover; drain. Combine bacon, onion and butter in a large saucepan and cook over medium heat until golden, stirring frequently.
❧ Add the celery, carrots, zucchini, red beans and potatoes, season with salt and pepper and cook, stirring, for 5 minutes. Add tomatoes, tomato paste, broth and green beans and bring to boil. Lower heat and simmer, covered, for 2 hours.
❧ Add rice and cook uncovered over high heat for 5 minutes.
❧ Pour soup into bowls and stir 1 tablespoon Parmesan into each. Cool completely and sprinkle with parsley before serving.

Serves 6

Toscana

GINESTRATA
SWEET AND SOUR CREAM SOUP

This is a delicate soup typical of the Chianti area. Like all the sweet and sour dishes found in Italian cooking, it is a very old recipe. The soup has a creamy consistency and is served in small quantities because it is very filling.

pinch of ground cinnamon
pinch of grated nutmeg
1 tablespoon sugar
6 egg yolks
pinch of salt

6 cups (48 fl oz/1.5 l) chicken broth (stock)
½ cup (4 fl oz/125 ml) *vin santo* or
 sweet white wine
3 tablespoons unsalted butter

Mix together the cinnamon, nutmeg and sugar. Beat the eggs in a saucepan. Add the salt, broth and *vin santo*. Stir in the butter; continue stirring over moderate heat until the soup thickens. Do not boil or the eggs will curdle.

Pour soup into cups, sprinkle with the spice mixture and serve.

Serves 6

SWEET AND SOUR CREAM SOUP

Toscana

RISO ALLA TOSCANA
TUSCAN RICE

Tuscany is one of the richest vegetable growing areas of Italy. For this reason, vegetables are featured in many dishes both as part of the ingredients and as garnishes.

3 cups (1¼ lb/625 g) Arborio rice
1 lb (500 g) zucchini, chopped
2 oz (60 g) zucchini flowers, pistils removed
½ cup (4 oz/125 g) unsalted butter, melted
2 tablespoons chopped parsley

☙ Cook the rice in plenty of boiling salted water until *al dente;* drain.
☙ Meanwhile, sauté the zucchini and half of the flowers in ¼ cup (2 oz/60 g) butter over high heat for 2 minutes. Add to rice with the remaining butter and the parsley.
☙ Place the rice in a mold just large enough to hold it. Press down lightly, then turn out onto a serving plate and garnish with the remaining flowers.

Serves 6   *Photograph page 6*

Toscana

CACIUCCO ALLA LIVORNESE
LIVORNO FISH STEW

Livorno, or Leghorn, is a city by the sea, famous for its beautiful seventeenth-century port, its naval academy, and its fish soup called caciucco, *of which crustaceans and mollusks are essential ingredients.*

½ cup (4 fl oz/125 ml) extra virgin olive oil
1 onion, finely chopped
1 carrot, finely chopped
1 celery stalk, finely chopped
½ cup (¾ oz/20 g) chopped parsley
a small piece of hot red chili pepper, minced
1 small lobster, in shell
1 lb (500 g) large shrimp (king prawns),
   in their shells
1 medium cuttlefish or squid, cleaned and
   sliced into rings
10 oz (315 g) octopus, cut into small pieces
1 cup (8 fl oz/250 ml) dry white wine
½ cup (4 fl oz/125 ml) hot water
10 oz (315 g) plum (egg) tomatoes, put
   through a food mill
salt
1 lb (500 g) fresh mussels
1 lb (500 g) fresh clams
2 red mullet or small red snapper, filleted
   and cut into pieces
1¼ lb (625 g) fillets of white-fleshed fish
   (scorpionfish or bream), cut into pieces
10 oz (315 g) dogfish or shark, cut
   into pieces
8 thin slices of firm, coarse-textured bread
2 garlic cloves, halved and crushed

☙ Heat the oil in a large saucepan over moderate heat. Add the onion, carrot, celery, parsley and chili pepper and cook until onion begins to color. Add the lobster, shrimp, squid and octopus and mix well. Cook gently for 10 minutes. Pour in the wine and hot water.
☙ Remove the lobster and shrimp, add the tomatoes and simmer for 10 minutes. Season with salt. Remove all the seafood and set aside.
☙ Steam the mussels and clams in another

large saucepan of water over moderate heat just until open. Strain the cooking liquid and add it to the soup. Add all the remaining fish and simmer until opaque. Return the reserved seafood to the stew.

Meanwhile, toast the bread slices and rub with the garlic. Place in the bottom of a soup tureen. Pour in the fish stew and serve very hot.

Serves 8

RICE-STUFFED TOMATOES

Lazio

POMODORI RIPIENI DI RISO

RICE-STUFFED TOMATOES

Tomatoes filled with rice are one of the most popular summer dishes in Rome. They may be eaten hot, but they are often also served cold. The important thing is to use tomatoes that are very ripe and not watery, and to use lots of herbs to flavor them. In winter they may be flavored with plenty of dried oregano.

6 good-sized ripe tomatoes
½ cup (3½ oz/110 g) Arborio rice
1 tablespoon chopped fresh oregano
1 tablespoon chopped fresh marjoram
1 tablespoon chopped fresh mint
1 tablespoon chopped parsley
¼ cup (2 fl oz/60 ml) extra virgin olive oil
salt and freshly ground pepper

🌿 Cut a slice from the top of each tomato to make a cap. Carefully hollow out the tomato and sieve the flesh into a bowl. Add the rice, herbs, 3 tablespoons oil, salt and pepper and let stand for about 30 minutes to blend the flavors.

🌿 Meanwhile, sprinkle the insides of the tomatoes with salt and turn them upside down to drain out their moisture.

🌿 Preheat an oven to 350°F (180°C). Drain the rice, reserving the tomato liquid. Fill the tomatoes with the rice and pour a little tomato liquid on top of each. Replace the caps on the tomatoes and arrange in a baking dish that has been brushed with the remaining oil. Bake for 1 hour or until the rice is tender and dry, gradually adding the reserved tomato liquid until it is absorbed.

Serves 6

Liguria

TORTA DI VERDURA
VEGETABLE TART

Liguria is famous for its vegetables and for the many wild herbs that are used in its stuffings, sauces and soups. The oil used is almost always extra virgin olive oil, which is produced in particular in the area around Imperia.

1⅔ cups (8 oz/250 g) all-purpose (plain) flour
½ cup (4 fl oz/125 ml) extra virgin olive oil
3 eggs
salt
a handful (¼ cup) dried *porcini* (boletus) mushrooms or champignons
1 onion, chopped
6 anchovy fillets in oil
1 lb (500 g) beet greens or spinach leaves, shredded
2 tablespoons chopped fresh marjoram
2 tablespoons water
freshly ground pepper
3 oz (90 g) ricotta

🕸 Heap flour in a mound on a board and make a well in the center. Add ¼ cup (2 fl oz/ 60 ml) oil, 1 egg and a pinch of salt to the well, then work in enough water to make a soft dough. Knead until smooth and elastic. Cover with a cloth and let rest.

🕸 Soak mushrooms in lukewarm water for about 30 minutes; drain and chop coarsely.

🕸 Heat remaining oil in a saucepan and sauté onion over low heat until translucent. Add anchovies, beet greens, marjoram, mushrooms and 2 tablespoons water. Season with salt and pepper, cover and simmer for 10 minutes.

🕸 Remove from heat. Beat remaining 2 eggs with ricotta, add to saucepan and mix well. Let filling cool.

🕸 Preheat an oven to 350°F (180°C). Roll out dough and use it to line a buttered 10-in (25-cm) tart pan. Spread with prepared filling. Bake the tart in the oven for about 40 minutes. Serve hot.

Serves 4–6

VEGETABLE TART

Lombardia

RISOTTO ALLO ZAFFERANO
SAFFRON RICE

The best-flavored saffron is produced in the Abruzzi near the town of l'Aquila; in Sardinia; and in Kashmir. The most highly prized is in thread form—the intact pistils of the crocus from which saffron is harvested—but it is more commonly found powdered. Rice with saffron is also known as risotto alla milanese *because it is a traditional specialty of Milan.*

⅓ cup (3 oz/90 g) unsalted butter
½ cup (4 oz/125 g) beef marrow
1 small onion, finely chopped
2 cups (13 oz/410 g) Arborio rice
½ cup (4 fl oz/125 ml) dry white wine
6 cups (48 fl oz/1.5 l) meat broth (stock), boiling
¼ teaspoon saffron
1 cup (4 oz/125 g) freshly grated Parmesan cheese
salt and freshly ground pepper

☙ Melt half the butter and the marrow in a deep skillet over moderate heat. Add onion and sauté until translucent.
☙ Add rice and stir for 2 minutes. Pour in wine and cook until it evaporates. Add boiling broth ½ cup at a time, stirring constantly until each addition is absorbed before adding the next. The rice should always be covered by a "veil" of broth.
☙ Add saffron, dissolved in a little broth. When rice is cooked to porridge consistency—

after about 15 minutes—add Parmesan cheese, remaining butter, and salt and pepper to taste. Cover and let *risotto* rest for a few minutes before serving.

Serves 6

Friuli - Venezia Giulia

POLENTA E SALSICCIA
POLENTA AND SAUSAGES

Polenta, which in this region is finely ground, is the basis of many dishes. It is toasted under the broiler (grill), served in slices with mountain cheese, or eaten with stewed pork, salami slices or oven-baked sausages.

6 cups (48 fl oz/1.5 l) water
salt
2⅔ cups (13 oz/410 g) fine cornmeal
1½ lb (750 g) Italian sausages
3 tablespoons unsalted butter
1 tablespoon red wine vinegar

☙ Bring water to boil in a large saucepan with a generous pinch of salt. Sprinkle in cornmeal, stirring constantly with a wooden spoon. Cook for 40 minutes, stirring frequently.
☙ Prick the sausages with a fork. Melt butter in a cast iron skillet. Add sausages and fry slowly for 10 minutes, turning from time to time. When they are cooked, drizzle vinegar over them and let it evaporate.
☙ Spoon polenta onto a serving plate. Top with sausages and spoon melted sausage fat over it. Serve at once.

Serves 6

SAFFRON RICE (TOP LEFT) AND
POLENTA AND SAUSAGES (BOTTOM)

POTATO PIE

Puglia

TORTA TARANTINA
POTATO PIE

In this potato pie, which resembles pizza, mozzarella cheese and anchovies are used for added flavor. It is very similar to the potato "gâteau" (gattò di patate) prepared in middle-class Neapolitan kitchens; this, however, is filled with mozzarella and ham.

2 lb (1 kg) baking potatoes
1 can (1 lb/500 g) peeled tomatoes, chopped
salt
¼ cup (2 fl oz/60 ml) extra virgin olive oil
freshly ground pepper
10 oz (315 g) mozzarella, sliced
8 anchovy fillets in oil, chopped
1 teaspoon dried oregano
chopped parsley (optional)

Boil the potatoes in their skins in salted water until tender. Place the tomatoes in a colander and sprinkle heavily with salt. Allow to drain for 10 to 15 minutes to rid them of as much moisture as possible.

Peel the potatoes and force through a sieve. Mix in half the oil and salt and pepper to taste.

Oil a round pizza tray and spread the potato mixture over it. Arrange the mozzarella slices on the potato layer and scatter the anchovies on top.

Preheat an oven to 400°F (200°C). Arrange the tomato over the potatoes, sprinkle with the oregano and drizzle the rest of the oil over. Bake for 20 minutes. Serve hot, sprinkled with chopped parsley if desired.

Serves 4–6

Campania

PIZZA MARGHERITA
TRADITIONAL PIZZA

Pizza dough forms a base for a great variety of toppings, from the simplest—such as garlic and oregano—to seafood, different cheeses or vegetables. The margherita *is perhaps the most traditional version.*

1 oz (30 g) fresh yeast or 1 envelope dry yeast
3¼ cups (1 lb/500 g) all-purpose (plain) flour
1 lb (500 g) plum (egg) tomatoes, peeled and cut into thin wedges
10 oz (315 g) mozzarella, sliced
1 tablespoon chopped fresh oregano or 1½ teaspoons dried oregano
¼ cup (2 fl oz/60 ml) extra virgin olive oil

Dissolve the yeast in ½ cup (4 fl oz/ 125 ml) warm water. Heap the flour in a mound on a board, make a well in the center and pour in the dissolved yeast. Add enough extra water to form a soft dough. Knead until smooth and elastic. Cover the dough with a towel and let rise in a large bowl until doubled in volume.

Press and stretch dough out in a circle ⅜ in (1 cm) thick on a floured board with the fingertips; do not use a rolling pin.

Flour a baking sheet and place the dough onto it. Cover the pizza base with the mozzarella slices, top with tomato, sprinkle with oregano and drizzle the oil over. Bake in a preheated 450°F (230°C) oven until the crust is lightly browned, about 20 minutes. Serve hot.

Serves 4–6

TRADITIONAL PIZZA

Friuli - Venezia Giulia

GNOCCHI DI PRUGNE
PRUNE GNOCCHI

This dish, Austrian in origin, is popular among the families of Trieste. Austrian influence is still very evident in the Venezia Giulia region, particularly in the big families that at one time were often connected by birth to the Austro-Hungarian Empire.

12 dried prunes
2 lb (1 kg) baking potatoes
2 cups (10 oz/315 g) all-purpose (plain) flour
1 egg
salt
⅓ cup (3 oz/90 g) unsalted butter
1 cup (2 oz/60 g) fresh breadcrumbs
pinch of ground cloves

Soak prunes in lukewarm water for 1 hour. Drain, pit and cut into small pieces. Set aside.

Boil the potatoes in their skins until tender. Drain and peel them. Force through a sieve; mix with ⅔ of the flour, the egg and a pinch of salt.

Knead the potato mixture well with floured hands. Form it into oval gnocchi about 1 in (2.5 cm) long. Insert a piece of prune into each and close the mixture over it. Arrange the gnocchi in rows on a floured board.

Bring a large saucepan of salted water to boil. Cook the gnocchi a few at a time, lifting them out with a slotted spoon as they rise to the surface. Arrange on a serving dish.

Heat half the butter in a skillet. Fry the breadcrumbs with the cloves until they begin to color. Brown the remaining butter in a small skillet. Drizzle over the gnocchi, scatter with breadcrumbs and serve.

Serves 4–6

Emilia - Romagna

MALFATTI DI RICOTTA
RICOTTA GNOCCHI

These gnocchi are called malfatti *("badly made") because they are shaped by hand and therefore are irregular in appearance. They may be prepared ahead and covered with bechamel sauce that has been flavored with a few sliced* porcini *(boletus) mushrooms, then baked until heated through.*

2 cups chopped cooked spinach (made from 2 lb/1 kg fresh spinach)
2 cups (8 oz/250 g) freshly grated Parmesan cheese
⅓ cup (2 oz/60 g) all-purpose (plain) flour
1 cup (8 oz/250 g) ricotta cheese
2 eggs
pinch of grated nutmeg
salt and freshly ground pepper
⅓ cup (3 oz/90 g) unsalted butter, melted

In a large mixing bowl, combine the spinach with ½ cup (2 oz/60 g) of the Parmesan, ¼ cup (1½ oz/45 g) flour, ricotta, eggs, nutmeg and salt and pepper to taste. Mix well.

With the help of a spoon, shape the spinach mixture into ovals about the size of a walnut and roll each one in the remaining flour.

Bring a pot of lightly salted water to boil. Drop the gnocchi a few at a time into the boiling water and cook until they float to the surface. Drain in a colander and arrange on the serving dish. Pour the melted butter over the gnocchi, sprinkle with the remaining Parmesan and serve.

Serves 4–6

PRUNE GNOCCHI (TOP) AND RICOTTA GNOCCHI (BOTTOM)

WIDE RIBBON NOODLES WITH HARE SAUCE

Toscana

PAPPARDELLE ALLA LEPRE
WIDE RIBBON NOODLES WITH HARE SAUCE

The Tuscans are great hunters, and in autumn they love to eat game—hare, pheasant, even wild boar. They serve it roasted and stewed and make marvelous game sauces for pasta or rice.

1¼ lb (625 g) hare or rabbit meat
1 cup (8 fl oz/250 ml) dry red wine
2 fresh rosemary sprigs
salt
½ cup (4 fl oz/125 ml) extra virgin olive oil
1 small onion, chopped
1 garlic clove, chopped
1 celery stalk, chopped
2 bay leaves
1 tablespoon juniper berries
freshly ground pepper
1 tablespoon tomato paste (purée)
1⅓ cups (7 oz/220 g) all-purpose (plain) flour
2 eggs
½ cup (2 oz/60 g) freshly grated Parmesan
    cheese

⚜ Cut the hare into pieces and place in a bowl. Add the wine and rosemary and marinate for 24 hours.

⚜ Drain the meat, reserving the wine. Place meat in a saucepan with a little salt. Cover and cook over low heat for 10 minutes, then pour off the accumulated liquid. Add the oil, onion, garlic, celery, bay leaves, juniper berries and pepper and cook over moderate heat until onion begins to color, 10 to 15 minutes, stirring constantly.

🌣 Pour in the wine and let it evaporate. Add the tomato paste, diluted with a little water, and simmer uncovered for about 1½ hours, adding water as necessary to keep the sauce moist.

🌣 Meanwhile, mound the flour on a work surface and make a well in the center. Break the eggs into the well and mix with your hands to form a dough. Knead until smooth and elastic. Roll out the dough thinly and cut into strips 1-in (2.5-cm) wide.

🌣 Discard the bay leaves from the sauce. Bone the meat and chop it coarsely. Return it to the saucepan and reheat, adding more water if required to reach sauce consistency.

🌣 Cook the *pappardelle* noodles in boiling salted water until *al dente,* about 2–3 minutes. Drain and toss with the sauce. Sprinkle with Parmesan and serve.

Serves 6

Friuli - Venezia Giulia

CIALSONS
PASTA WITH HERBS

Cialsons, *little semicircles of filled pasta, are very popular in Friuli. They may be filled in various ways: the most traditional stuffing is based on herbs, but they are also delicious with a filling of spinach, golden raisins (sultanas), cinnamon, a small amount of softened rye bread, and poppyseeds. They are served with a sauce of melted butter and grated aged ricotta, or grated Parmesan cheese.*

1⅓ cups (7 oz/220 g) all-purpose (plain) flour

3 eggs

3½ cups (7 oz/220 g) beet greens or spinach leaves

¼ cup (1 oz/30 g) stale rye breadcrumbs, soaked in milk and squeezed dry

pinch of ground cinnamon

pinch of ground cloves

1 tablespoon chopped fresh thyme

1 tablespoon chopped parsley

1 tablespoon juniper berries, ground

salt and freshly ground pepper

⅓ cup (3 oz/90 g) unsalted butter, melted

¾ cup (3 oz/90 g) freshly grated Parmesan cheese

🌣 Heap the flour on a board and make a well in the center. Break 2 eggs into the well and gradually work in flour. Knead until dough is smooth and elastic. Cover while preparing filling.

🌣 Boil the beet or spinach leaves in salted water just until wilted. Squeeze dry and chop finely. Mix with remaining egg, the bread, cinnamon, cloves, thyme, parsley and juniper berries. Season to taste with salt and pepper.

🌣 Roll dough out into thin sheets and cut into circles about 2 in (5 cm) in diameter.

🌣 Place little mounds of filling onto the pasta circles. Fold them in half to enclose the filling and press the edges together firmly.

🌣 Cook the *cialsons* in boiling salted water until *al dente,* about 2-3 minutes, and drizzle with the melted butter. Sprinkle grated Parmesan on top.

Serves 6   *Photograph pages 44–45*

Veneto

RAVIOLI DI BARBABIETOLE

BEET RAVIOLI

In Italy, beets (beetroot) can be found already cooked in most fruit and vegetable markets. Each evening the vendors bake at home as many beets as they think they will sell the following day. They also cook onions in their skins in the same manner. Baked beets and onions mixed with a dressing of oil and lemon make an excellent salad.

1⅓ cups (7 oz/220 g) all-purpose (plain) flour
salt
3 eggs
1 beet (beetroot), about 10 oz (315 g), baked at 350°F (180°C) until tender
⅓ cup (3 oz/90 g) unsalted butter
7 oz (220 g) ricotta
freshly ground pepper
½ cup (2 oz/50 g) dry breadcrumbs
¾ cup (3 oz/90 g) freshly grated Parmesan cheese

🌀 Sift the flour and a pinch of salt into a mound on a work surface. Make a well in the center and break 2 eggs into it. Work the flour into a soft dough. Form it into a ball, wrap in plastic and let it rest while you prepare the filling.

🌀 Peel and slice the beet; purée in a food processor. Melt 4 tablespoons (2 oz/60 g) butter in a saucepan. Add the beet and cook gently for about 10 minutes to gather flavor. Transfer to a bowl and blend in the ricotta, the remaining egg and the breadcrumbs. Adjust the salt and add pepper.

🌀 Roll out the dough as thinly as possible with a rolling pin or pasta machine. Cut into circles about 2 in (5 cm) in diameter. Place a little of the beet mixture in the center of each circle. Fold the pasta over the filling and press edges firmly.

🌀 Bring a large saucepan of water to boil and cook the ravioli in it until *al dente*, about 2–3 minutes.

🌀 Meanwhile, heat the remaining butter in a small saucepan until fairly dark in color. Drain the ravioli and place on a serving plate. Pour the melted butter over, sprinkle with cheese and serve.

Serves 6   *Photograph pages 44–45*

Toscana

PANZANELLA

BREAD SALAD WITH TOMATO

This is another traditional recipe that makes use of leftover bread; it is mixed with tomatoes, onions and olive oil, and sometimes other ingredients such as tuna and olives are added. Because Tuscan bread is unsalted it stays fresh longer than bread that contains salt.

8 oz (250 g) week-old firm, coarse-textured bread
3 large ripe tomatoes, peeled and cut into cubes
2 small red onions, minced
4 garlic cloves, chopped
⅓ cup (⅓ oz/10 g) whole fresh basil leaves
3 oz (90 g) canned tuna, drained
2 tablespoons red wine vinegar
salt
⅓ cup (3 fl oz/90 ml) extra virgin olive oil
freshly ground pepper

◈ Soak the bread in water for a few minutes. Squeeze dry and crumble into a mixing bowl.

◈ Mix the tomatoes, onions, garlic, basil and tuna with the bread.

◈ In a small bowl, mix the vinegar with a pinch of salt until the salt is dissolved. Whisk in the olive oil. Toss with the salad, salt and pepper to taste and serve.

Serves 6   *Photograph page 6*

Liguria

TRENETTE AL PESTO
TRENETTE WITH PESTO

Genoese pesto sauce is usually made in a marble mortar by pounding the basil leaves with the rest of the ingredients using a wooden pestle. This prevents the basil from turning black with the heat of the pasta (a reaction usually set off by the steel in a cutting knife). In the absence of a mortar pesto can be made in a blender. Trenette are fine ribbon noodles, which can be made at home with 2½ cups (13 oz/410 g) flour, two eggs, and sufficient water to make a soft, smooth dough. Ligurian pasta, unlike that of other regions, contains only a small proportion of egg and is almost white in color.

1 cup (1 oz/30 g) fresh basil leaves, tightly packed
2 tablespoons pine nuts
3 garlic cloves, peeled
salt
3 tablespoons grated pecorino cheese
3 tablespoons freshly grated Parmesan cheese
½ cup (4 fl oz/125 ml) extra virgin olive oil

TRENETTE WITH PESTO

2 boiling potatoes
1 lb (500 g) green beans, trimmed
13 oz (410 g) *trenette*

◈ Wash the basil leaves and dry them well.

◈ Combine pine nuts, garlic and basil in a blender. Add a little salt, the cheeses and a small amount of oil, and purée. Pour in remaining oil and blend for a further second or two. Peel the potatoes and cut into julienne strips.

◈ Bring a large saucepan of water to boil, drop in beans and cook for 5 minutes. Add the potatoes, and after 2 minutes add the noodles. When noodles are cooked *al dente*, about 5 minutes, drain mixture and turn out onto a serving plate. Toss with the prepared pesto and serve.

Serves 4

AGNOLOTTI ALLA PANNA

AGNOLOTTI WITH CREAM

Stuffed pasta comes in many different forms and under many different names, which all amount to the same thing: agnolotti *in Piedmont,* ravioli *in Tuscany,* tortelli *and* cappelletti *in Emilia-Romagna,* pansoti *in Liguria. They can be half-moon shaped, square, hat-shaped or round, and they are filled with a meat mixture, vegetables, eggs or cheese.*

FILLING

10 cups (10 oz/315 g) young beet greens or spinach leaves

3 oz (90 g) ricotta

3 oz (90 g) leftover roast chicken, finely chopped

3 oz (90 g) cooked ham, finely chopped

¼ cup (1 oz/30 g) freshly grated Parmesan cheese

1 egg

pinch of freshly grated nutmeg

salt and freshly ground pepper

PASTA

2 cups (10 oz/315 g) all-purpose (plain) flour

3 eggs

SAUCE

3 tablespoons unsalted butter

1 cup (8 fl oz/250 ml) cream

¾ cup (3 oz/90 g) freshly grated Parmesan cheese

To prepare the filling: cook the beet or spinach leaves in boiling salted water just until wilted. Squeeze dry and chop very finely. In a bowl, combine all of the filling ingredients. Refrigerate.

To prepare the pasta: combine flour and eggs to form a dough; knead until smooth and elastic. Roll out very thinly. Place small balls of the filling at 2½-in (6-cm) intervals over half the sheet of dough. Fold the dough

over to cover filling, pressing with the fingers around each ball. Using a pastry wheel with fluted edge, cut out the *agnolotti* in half-moon or square shapes.

Bring a large pot of water to boil over high heat; drop in the *agnolotti* and cook until *al dente,* about 2–3 minutes.

To prepare the sauce: while the *agnolotti* are cooking, heat the butter and cream over low heat. Arrange *agnolotti* in a serving dish and pour butter and cream over. Sprinkle with Parmesan and serve.

Serves 6

Piemonte

GNOCCHI DI PATATE

POTATO GNOCCHI

Potato gnocchi are a Piedmontese specialty, but they are also found in the cuisine of many other northern regions and in Latium. They may be served with meat sauce, pesto, sage leaves fried in butter, tomato sauce or a rich sauce made by melting gorgonzola cheese with a little butter and cream.

RAGÙ

1 carrot

1 celery stalk

1 small onion

10 oz (315 g) fresh or canned tomatoes, peeled and seeded

2 oz (60 g) *pancetta* or rindless bacon

⅓ cup (3 oz/90 g) unsalted butter

10 oz (315 g) beef tenderloin (fillet), cut into cubes

¼ cup (2 fl oz/60 ml) dry white wine

salt and freshly ground pepper

1 cup (4 oz/125 g) freshly grated Parmesan cheese

GNOCCHI

2 lb (1 kg) baking potatoes

1⅓ cups (7 oz/220 g) all-purpose (plain) flour

1 egg

salt

To prepare the sauce: cut the vegetables and bacon into small pieces. Melt 1 tablespoon butter in a saucepan. Add the carrot, celery, onion and meat, browning the meat over medium-high heat. Reduce heat to medium and cook for 10 minutes more. Add the wine and tomatoes, season to taste with salt

and pepper, and cook over very low heat for 2 hours. Push the sauce through a sieve—do not purée.

To prepare the gnocchi: boil the potatoes in their skins until tender. Drain and peel them. Put potatoes through a food mill held over a board or other work surface or mash potatoes well. Add the flour, gather the mixture into a mound and make a well in the center. Break the egg into the well, add salt and knead until the mixture forms a smooth, firm dough.

Cut it into pieces and use the palm of your hand to roll each piece into a long sausage shape. Cut these into 2¼-in (3-cm) cylinders, separating them. Roll each of the gnocchi over the concave part of a grater or the prongs of a fork, pressing down lightly with your thumb, and drop them onto a floured board.

Cook the gnocchi a few at a time in boiling salted water, lifting them out with a slotted spoon as soon as they rise to the surface. Spoon the sauce over them, dot with the remaining butter and sprinkle with Parmesan. Serve at once.

Serves 4–6 *Photograph page 20*

Puglia

PENNE CON I BROCCOLI

PASTA WITH BROCCOLI

In summer, when broccoli (normally an autumn vegetable) is not available, this dish can be made with swiss chard or beet greens. Housewives in Italy prefer to buy only vegetables that are in season, thinking, quite rightly, that they have more flavor.

¼ cup (1 oz/30 g) raisins
½ cup (4 fl oz/125 ml) extra virgin olive oil
½ onion, chopped
1 can (1 lb/500 g) peeled tomatoes, sieved
salt and freshly ground pepper
2 lb (1 kg) broccoli
13 oz (410 g) *penne* (straight pasta tubes)
6 anchovy fillets in oil, mashed
2 garlic cloves, chopped
⅓ cup (1½ oz/45 g) pine nuts
⅓ cup (1½ oz/40 g) grated pecorino cheese

Soak the raisins in lukewarm water to cover until needed. Heat half the oil in a skillet over moderate heat. Add the onion and sauté until translucent. Add the tomatoes, season with salt and pepper, cover and cook for about 1 hour to reduce the sauce.

Meanwhile, separate the broccoli into florets and stems. Peel and slice the stems. Drop into a saucepan of boiling salted water with *penne* and cook until *al dente,* about 4–5 minutes.

Fry the anchovy fillets gently with the garlic in oil until garlic is fragrant. Add to the tomato sauce. Mix in the drained raisins and pine nuts and cook sauce over low heat for 5 minutes, stirring frequently.

Pour sauce over the cooked pasta and broccoli and mix well. Sprinkle with the grated cheese. Serve at once.

Serves 6

PASTA WITH BROCCOLI

SPAGHETTI WITH EGGS AND BACON

Lazio

SPAGHETTI ALLA CARBONARA
SPAGHETTI WITH EGGS AND BACON

In the south of Italy tagliatelle is replaced by spaghetti, which requires a different sauce. Tagliatelle is generally served with butter-based sauces, spaghetti with sauces based on extra virgin olive oil or using some form of bacon or salt pork.

10 oz (310 g) *pancetta* or rindless bacon, finely diced
1 hot red chili pepper, finely chopped
1¼ lb (600 g) spaghetti
⅓ cup (1½ oz/40 g) grated pecorino cheese
6 egg yolks (see glossary)
salt and freshly ground pepper
3 tablespoons freshly grated Parmesan cheese

Combine the *pancetta* and chili pepper in a skillet and cook over low heat until some of the fat has melted. Increase the heat and cook until the *pancetta* browns.

Bring a large pot of salted water to boil and cook the spaghetti in it until *al dente,* about 4–5 minutes. Drain, reserving ½ cup water. Transfer to a serving dish.

Mix the pecorino with the reserved spaghetti cooking water. Mix in the egg yolks with a fork, then add a little salt and plenty of pepper. Tip the contents of the skillet over the spaghetti. Add the egg mixture and toss well. Sprinkle with Parmesan and serve.

Serves 6

Campania

SPAGHETTI ALLE VONGOLE
SPAGHETTI WITH CLAM SAUCE

This sauce may be prepared with or without tomatoes. If tomatoes are used, 1 lb (500 g) are added to the oil and garlic and left to reduce for 1 hour. The opened clams are added to the sauce with the reduced clam liquid for the last five minutes of cooking.

4 lb (2 kg) clams in the shell or 18 oz (560 g) canned baby clams in water, drained and liquid reserved
freshly ground pepper
½ cup (4 fl oz/125 ml) extra virgin olive oil
6 garlic cloves, chopped
salt
13 oz (410 g) spaghetti
¼ cup (⅓ oz/10 g) chopped parsley

SPAGHETTI WITH CLAM SAUCE

Scrub the clams well and rinse them. Place in a large skillet over moderate heat until all the shells have opened; discard any unopened clams. Lift clams from the pan with a slotted spoon, set aside and keep warm.

Strain the liquid left in the pan and return it to the heat. Add pepper and cook the liquid over fairly high heat until reduced to ¼ cup (2 fl oz/60 ml).

Pour the oil into a small skillet, add the garlic and fry gently until golden. At the same time, bring a large saucepan of salted water to boil, add spaghetti and cook until *al dente,* about 4–5 minutes.

Drain the spaghetti and place in a serving bowl. Toss with the oil, garlic and clam cooking liquid. Scatter the clams on top, sprinkle with chopped parsley and serve.

Serves 6

I SECONDI

IN THE DEVELOPMENT of meal planning over the centuries, the greatest importance has been attached to the second course, or what Italians know as *il secondo,* sometimes formally referred to as an "entree." If we imagine a dinner as being represented by a graph, the line would begin at the *antipasto* and rise gradually through the first course, to reach a peak at the main course and descend again with desserts. As menus have become progressively simpler, for practical reasons, there has been a tendency for *antipasti,* first courses and desserts to disappear, while the main course with its accompaniments has been elevated to the dignity of a complete repast.

We should clarify that we are referring to meat, not to fish, because until a few decades ago fish was permitted at the table only on Friday, a day of fasting and purification; it was considered a humble food unworthy of important guests. A meat dish—beef in particular—was seen as a tangible demonstration of the esteem in which a guest was held.

Meat is categorized as white, red or black. White meat includes veal, lamb, suckling pig, poultry and rabbit; red meat includes beef, pork and mutton; black meat refers to game. In general, the choicest pieces for roasting and grilling come from the leg and back portions of the animal, while the best cuts

for stewing, boiling and frying are from the front and sides of the beast. Meat should be left at room temperature for at least an hour before cooking so that the fibers are not stiff from the cold. It should not be prepared on a wooden board, because the wood tends to draw out the juices. For the same reason it should never be salted when raw, but only halfway through cooking.

As for fish, it is best to concentrate on varieties that are in season and therefore fresh and cheap. Red gills, firm flesh, and bright eyes that show no signs of being sunken are the visible indications of freshness, which is essential. Fish should never on any account be kept in the refrigerator for more than eight hours; if it is necessary to keep them for a longer period, they should be sprinkled with coarse salt, wrapped in foil and frozen.

Finally, for the main course there is that marvelous resource, the egg. A *tortino* or *frittata* prepared with imagination can proudly be served to guests as long as it is evident that a certain amount of thought and effort have gone into it. Fresh eggs should be taken from the refrigerator before use and brought to room temperature. Break your eggs into a bowl, add a pinch of salt, and whisk them for a few minutes with a fork. With the addition of *porcini* mushrooms, *ovoli* or, better still, truffles, a *frittata* makes a first-class main dish.

PORK LIVER WITH FENNEL (TOP, RECIPE PAGE 72), PORK SAUSAGE WITH LENTILS (BOTTOM RIGHT, RECIPE PAGE 72) AND STEWED BABY OCTOPI (BOTTOM LEFT, RECIPE PAGE 58)

DEEP-FRIED MOZZARELLA

Campania

MOZZARELLA IN CARROZZA

DEEP-FRIED MOZZARELLA

The traditional mozzarella is made with buffalo milk. It is produced mainly in the Salerno region and in the area around Caserta, where a few herds of buffalo may still be found. Mozzarella sold commercially is now almost always made from cow's milk.

2 eggs
salt
12 slices of firm, coarse-textured bread
   without crust, about ⅜ in (1 cm) thick
6 anchovy fillets packed in salt, rinsed
6 mozzarella slices, the same size as the bread
   and about ⅜ in (1 cm) thick
1 cup (8 fl oz/250 ml) milk
¾ cup (4 oz/125 g) all-purpose (plain) flour
oil for frying

Beat eggs with salt in a wide dish. Line up the slices of bread on a work surface and place an anchovy fillet and a slice of mozzarella on 6 of them. Top with the remaining 6 bread slices. Dip the sandwiches quickly in the milk and then in the flour, then soak them for a few seconds in the beaten egg.

Heat ½ in (1 cm) of oil in a skillet until smoking. Add sandwiches and fry on both sides until golden. Drain on paper towels and serve immediately.

Serves 6

PARMIGIANA DI MELANZANE
BAKED EGGPLANT WITH MOZZARELLA

This is perhaps one of the most famous dishes of southern Italy—typical of the Campania region, but also popular in Sicily. It is a pan-Mediterranean dish; similar versions are to be found in Yugoslavia, Greece and Turkey.

2 lb (1 kg) eggplants (aubergines)
salt
oil for frying
4 garlic cloves, peeled and crushed
¼ cup (2 fl oz/60 ml) extra virgin olive oil
2 lb (1 kg) ripe tomatoes, peeled and chopped
freshly ground pepper
10 oz (315 g) mozzarella, sliced
¼ cup (⅓ oz/10 g) chopped fresh basil leaves

Wash the eggplants, cut off their tops and slice them crosswise, approximately ½ in (12 mm) thick. Sprinkle with salt and arrange the slices on a plate. Top with a weight and prop the plate at an angle so that most of the eggplant juices will drain out. Let drain for about 2 hours.

Dry the eggplant and fry in ½ in (1 cm) of smoking-hot oil until both sides are golden. Drain eggplant on paper towels.

Meanwhile, heat the garlic in the olive oil, add the peeled tomatoes and some salt and pepper, and cook this sauce for about 30 minutes to reduce it.

Preheat an oven to 400°F (200°C). Spread a couple of tablespoons of the tomato sauce in a baking dish. Add a layer of the eggplant slices and a few slices of mozzarella. Scatter some basil on top. Continue layering ingredients until all are used, finishing with a sprinkle of basil leaves. Bake in the oven for 20 minutes. Serve hot.

Serves 6

BAKED EGGPLANT WITH MOZZARELLA

Umbria

FRITTATA AI TARTUFI NERI
BLACK TRUFFLE FRITTATA

Black truffles are a specialty of Norcia, a small town in Umbria. They are used in stuffings or as a topping for pasta, served sliced over eggs cooked in butter, and added to pâtés—especially pâtés based on prosciutto. Although black truffles and the white truffles of Alba are harvested more or less at the same time of year, black truffles have a less intense flavor.

6 eggs
salt and freshly ground pepper
2 large baking potatoes, boiled, peeled
   and sliced
1 black truffle, diced
1 slice (3 oz/90 g) cooked prosciutto, diced
2 tablespoons extra virgin olive oil
additional black truffle, thinly sliced (optional)

❖ Beat the eggs with a little salt and pepper in a bowl. Stir in potatoes, truffle and prosciutto.
❖ Heat the oil in a nonstick skillet and pour in the egg mixture. When one side of the *frittata* has cooked, turn it with the aid of a flat lid, and finish cooking the second side. Transfer to a serving plate. If desired, scatter more sliced truffle on top of the *frittata* before serving.

Serves 6

Friuli - Venezia Giulia

FRITTATA ALLA VERDURA
VEGETABLE FRITTATA

Vegetable frittatas are very popular all year round. Here, as almost everywhere else in Italy, the vegetables used vary according to the season. In summer there are zucchini, peas and beans; in winter the popular radicchio, *fennel and celery.*

3 oz (90 g) sliced *pancetta* or rindless bacon
1¼ lb (625 g) *radicchio*, fennel, zucchini
   (courgettes) or spinach, cut into thin slices
   or small pieces
2 tablespoons extra virgin olive oil

VEGETABLE FRITTATA (LEFT) AND BLACK TRUFFLE FRITTATA (RIGHT)

salt and freshly ground pepper
6 eggs, beaten

Lay the *pancetta* slices in a cast iron skillet and cook over low heat until crisp. Remove from the pan and crumble, reserving the bacon fat.

In the oil over medium heat, cook the vegetable until it begins to wilt. Add salt and pepper and mix with eggs and bacon in a bowl.

Reheat the bacon fat in the skillet; pour egg mixture into the hot fat and cook on one side, then tip the *frittata* onto a flat lid and slide it back into the pan to cook the other side. Remove from heat while the center is still soft. Transfer the *frittata* to a serving plate and serve immediately.

Serves 6

Lombardia

INVOLTINI DI VERZA RIPIENI
STUFFED CABBAGE LEAVES

In winter, when cabbage leaves are tender, they are filled with a variety of the tastiest ingredients—sausages, meats of all kinds, prosciutto, mortadella—or simply with boiled rice flavored with herbs, Parmesan cheese and eggs to make a lighter vegetarian dish.

12 cabbage leaves
5 oz (155 g) ground (minced) pork
5 oz (155 g) ground (minced) beef
2 fresh pork sausages, peeled and mashed
½ cup (1 oz/30 g) fresh breadcrumbs, soaked in milk and squeezed dry
¾ cup (3 oz/90 g) freshly grated Parmesan cheese

STUFFED CABBAGE LEAVES

1 egg, beaten
1 sprig fresh thyme, chopped
2 tablespoons unsalted butter
salt and freshly ground pepper
¼ cup (2 fl oz/60 ml) light (single) cream or half and half (half milk and half cream)

🍴 Blanch the cabbage leaves for 1 minute in boiling salted water. Drain, lay flat on a cloth and press lightly on the stalks to flatten. Remove the hard, central stalk to make rolling easier.
🍴 Mix the pork, beef, sausage, breadcrumbs, Parmesan, egg and thyme. Spread this mixture on the cabbage leaves, roll them up and secure with a toothpick.
🍴 Melt the butter in a skillet and arrange the rolls in it. Cook over moderate heat for 20 minutes, turning them once very carefully and moistening them occasionally with a little water. Season with salt and pepper.
🍴 Pour the cream into the pan and boil until slightly thickened. Place the rolls on a plate, pour the cream over and serve immediately.

Serves 6

Sicilia

SARDE A BECCAFICO
SARDINES STUFFED WITH RAISINS AND PINE NUTS

In Sicilian cooking, raisins are often combined with fish as well as with meat. Sicily is known for the variety of grapes it produces, including the Pantelleria muscat, which is world famous for its sweetness.

2 lb (1 kg) fresh sardines
½ cup (3 oz/90 g) raisins
½ cup (3 oz/90 g) pine nuts

SARDINES STUFFED WITH RAISINS AND PINE NUTS

3 tablespoons fine dry breadcrumbs
2 garlic cloves, chopped
freshly ground pepper
2 tablespoons extra virgin olive oil
¾ cup (4 oz / 125 g) all-purpose (plain) flour
oil for frying

🐟 Clean and bone the sardines, remove the heads and tails, and wash and dry the fish.

🐟 Soak the raisins in a cup of lukewarm water until soft. Drain and pat dry. Mix raisins with the pine nuts, breadcrumbs, garlic, pepper and olive oil. Stuff the sardines with this mixture, then reclose them and coat thoroughly with flour.

🐟 Pour oil into skillet to the depth of 1 in (2.5 cm). Heat oil, then add the sardines and fry for 5 minutes or until nicely browned on both sides. Drain fish on paper towels and sprinkle with salt. Arrange on a dish and serve.

Serves 6

Liguria

SPIGOLA AL SALE
SEA BASS BAKED IN SALT

This method of cooking produces a particularly tasty fish that retains all its natural flavor. The fish used must be fairly large; salmon makes a good alternative to sea bass. The salt forms a hard crust around the fish that is easily broken away at the end of cooking.

1 4-lb (2-kg) sea bass, salmon or grouper, cleaned
3 fresh rosemary sprigs
salt and freshly ground pepper
8 lb (4 kg) coarse sea salt
¾ cup (4 oz/125 g) all-purpose (plain) flour
¼ cup (2 fl oz/60 ml) extra virgin olive oil
2 tablespoons unsalted butter
juice of 1 lemon
1 tablespoon chopped parsley

Preheat an oven to 400°F (200°C). Into the cavity of the fish put a sprig of rosemary and a sprinkle of salt and pepper. Cover the bottom of an oval casserole with half the sea salt and lay the fish on this, placing a sprig of rosemary underneath it and another on top. Cover the fish completely with the rest of the sea salt.

Mix the flour with a little water to make a thin paste. Brush the surface of the salt with the paste. Bake fish in the oven until the salt begins to brown, about 30 minutes.

Heat the oil and butter; before they begin to sizzle, stir in salt, pepper, lemon juice and parsley. Pour into a sauceboat. Bring casserole to the table and break the salt block. Remove

the fish and transfer to a serving dish. Serve the butter sauce with the fish.

Serves 6

Campania

POLPETIELLI AFFOGATI
STEWED BABY OCTOPI

Polpetielli *are tiny octopi weighing no more than 10 oz (315 g) each. This recipe is also sometimes used for baby squid or cuttlefish (ink removed); it may be served hot, lukewarm or cold. Whatever the seafood, it must be cooked for a long period over a very low flame. It is best to use a terracotta pan or casserole, which will diffuse the heat.*

2 lb (1 kg) baby octopi
salt
1 whole red chili pepper
1 tablespoon chopped parsley
1 small tomato, peeled and cut into strips
⅓ cup (3 fl oz/100 ml) extra virgin olive oil
1 lemon, cut into wedges

Remove the eyes, mouths and ink sacs from the octopi and discard; wash the octopi several times; do not dry. Beat them lightly with a mallet to tenderize. Place in a terracotta casserole and season with salt. Add the whole chili pepper, parsley, tomato and oil.

Cover tightly and cook over very low heat for 2 hours or until octopi are very tender. Remove from heat and let rest briefly.

Discard the chili pepper. Serve the octopi in the casserole, passing lemon wedges separately.

Serves 6　　　　*Photograph page 50*

MARINATED SWORDFISH

TEGLIA DI PESCE SPADA

MARINATED SWORDFISH

Swordfish is one of the most common Sicilian fish. It is caught mainly in the channel that divides Sicily from Africa and is sold fresh in the markets in autumn and winter. The fish is often grilled and served with oil, lemon juice and capers, which grow wild on the island and are preserved in salt.

6 swordfish steaks (or tuna steaks or snapper cutlets), about 7 oz (220 g) each
salt and freshly ground pepper
1 cup (8 fl oz/250 ml) dry white wine
1 fresh rosemary sprig
4 garlic cloves, finely chopped
¼ cup (2 fl oz/60 ml) extra virgin olive oil
2 tablespoons fine dry breadcrumbs

3 tablespoons drained capers, chopped
juice of 1 lemon

🐟 Place the swordfish steaks in a bowl and season with salt and pepper. Pour in the wine. Finely chop the rosemary leaves and add to fish with the garlic. Coat steaks well and marinate for at least 1 hour.

🐟 Drain fish, reserving marinade. Brush a skillet with oil and heat it. Sprinkle fish with breadcrumbs and capers, place in skillet and cook on both sides over medium heat until nearly cooked through, about 2–3 minutes per side, basting from time to time with marinade.

🐟 Whisk the rest of the oil with the lemon juice in a small bowl. Pour over the fish and cook for another 1–2 minutes. Serve hot.

Serves 6

Campania

FRITTO MISTO DI PESCE
MIXED FRIED SEAFOOD

This dish is usually made of tiny baby squid, cuttlefish rings and tails of scampi, or langoustines. It is served crisp and piping hot, garnished with lemon wedges and little sprigs of parsley.

10 oz (315 g) baby squid

10 oz (315 g) cuttlefish (or medium-large squid)

10 oz (315 g) scampi tails or large shrimp (prawns), shelled

¾ cup (4 oz/125 g) all-purpose (plain) flour

oil for deep frying

6 lemon wedges

salt

 Clean the squid and cuttlefish, removing the eyes, beaks and transparent quills. Leave the baby squid whole. Cut the bodies of the cuttlefish into rings and separate the tentacles.

 Wash all the seafood and dry it well. Dredge each piece in flour. Heat a good quantity of oil in a large cast iron skillet and fry the seafood a few pieces at a time. Drain on paper towels, sprinkle with salt and serve at once, accompanied with slices of lemon.

Serves 6

MIXED FRIED SEAFOOD

Lombardia

OSSI BUCHI IN GREMOLATA
STEWED VEAL SHANKS WITH LEMON

Gremolata is a mixture of parsley, anchovies and lemon rind traditionally sprinkled over these ossi buchi, *or veal shanks. The dish is generally served over saffron rice, which produces a perfect marriage of flavors. It is a good idea to ask the butcher to cut the meat from the central part of the shank, where the bone is smaller. The bone marrow is lifted out with a toothpick so that its taste can be savored.*

6 pieces veal shank *(ossi buchi)* cut about 1 in
   (2.5 cm) thick
¾ cup (4 oz/125 g) all-purpose (plain) flour
2 tablespoons unsalted butter
½ cup (4 fl oz/125 ml) dry white wine
salt and freshly ground pepper
1 anchovy fillet, chopped
juice of 1 lemon
grated rind of ½ lemon
2 tablespoons chopped parsley

STEWED VEAL SHANKS WITH LEMON

Dredge the veal shanks in flour, shaking off excess. Melt the butter in a wide skillet, arrange the veal shanks in it side by side, and brown them on one side over medium heat. Turn carefully and brown the other side.

Pour in the wine and allow to evaporate completely. Add salt and pepper, cover and simmer the meat for about 1½ hours, adding water a little at a time to keep some liquid in the bottom of the pan. Add the anchovy and the lemon juice and rind. Sprinkle with parsley and serve.

Serves 6

Lazio

SALTIMBOCCA ALLA ROMANA
VEAL SCALLOPS WITH PROSCIUTTO AND SAGE

Two versions of this dish are found in Latium: the veal may be rolled up around the ham, or the ham and sage may be placed on top of each piece of veal and secured with a toothpick before the scallops are cooked in butter and white wine.

6 slices prosciutto, halved
12 fresh sage leaves
12 veal scallops (escalopes) about 1½ lb (750 g)
1 tablespoon unsalted butter
½ cup (4 fl oz/125 ml) dry white wine
salt and freshly ground pepper

Place ½ slice of prosciutto and a sage leaf on each veal slice. Roll up each piece and secure with a toothpick.

Melt the butter in a heavy skillet and brown the veal rolls well. Add the white

VEAL WITH MARSALA SERVED WITH WHITE RICE (LEFT) AND VEAL SCALLOPS WITH PROSCIUTTO AND SAGE SERVED WITH CAULIFLOWER (RIGHT)

wine and cook until reduced to several tablespoons, scraping browned bits from the bottom of the pan. Cover and cook over low heat for 20 minutes, adding water a tablespoon or so at a time to keep meat from drying out. Serve rolls hot.

Serves 6

Lombardia

PICCATA AL MARSALA

VEAL WITH MARSALA

This piccata *is usually served on top of a Milanese risotto, (see* risotto alla zafferano, *page 35), making an elegant one-dish meal. This is one of the rare cases of rice being served with meat; it is normally not done. Another meat dish traditionally served with risotto is* ossi buchi in gremolata *(see page 62).*

1½ lb (750 g) veal rump roast, cut into 3-in (8-cm) round scallops (escalopes)
¾ cup (4 oz/125 g) all-purpose (plain) flour
3 tablespoons unsalted butter
salt and freshly ground pepper
½ cup (4 fl oz/125 ml) Marsala
1 tablespoon chopped parsley

Pound the meat until very thin. Dredge it in flour on both sides, shaking off excess. Melt the butter in a large skillet over high heat. Add the meat and brown on both sides. Season with salt and pepper. Pour in Marsala a little at a time.

Cover the skillet and cook over low heat for 25 minutes, adding water as needed to keep meat from drying out. Add parsley and cook 5 minutes longer. Serve immediately.

Serves 6

CALF'S LIVER VENETIAN STYLE

Veneto

FEGATO DI VITELLO ALLA VENEZIANA

CALF'S LIVER VENETIAN STYLE

It is essential for the success of this famous dish that the liver be tender and that it be cooked very briefly over very high heat, so that it does not become hard and dry. It is best to cook the onions separately and add them at the last moment.

1⅔ lb (800 g) calf's liver
5 onions, thinly sliced
3 tablespoons unsalted butter
½ cup (4 fl oz/125 ml) dry white wine

salt and freshly ground pepper
chopped parsley (optional)

🔥 Slice the liver very thinly, and cut into medium pieces. Fry the onions in half the butter in a skillet until golden. Add the wine and salt and pepper, cover and braise the onions until tender over low heat. Remove onions and keep warm.

🔥 Melt the rest of the butter in the skillet, add the liver and sauté over high heat just until cooked through. Add salt to taste, then mix in the onions. Serve immediately, garnished with chopped parsley if desired.

Serves 6

Lazio

CODA ALLA VACCINARA

OXTAIL RAGOUT

This simple but very tasty dish has a long cooking time so that all the fat in the oxtail can melt out gradually. The oxtail stock, strained and clarified, makes excellent aspic.

4 lb (2 kg) oxtail pieces
2 carrots
1 celery stalk, cut into several pieces
2 medium onions
¼ cup (⅓ oz/10 g) chopped parsley
2 bay leaves
2 oz (60 g) fatty prosciutto
2 tablespoons extra virgin olive oil
salt and freshly ground pepper
¾ cup (6 fl oz/200 ml) dry white wine
1 lb (500 g) peeled tomatoes

1 fresh thyme sprig
2 whole cloves
pinch of lemon peel

🔥 Combine oxtail, 1 carrot, celery, 1 onion and parsley in a large saucepan. Add enough salted water so that the pieces of meat float.

🔥 Bring to boil; simmer over low heat for 4 hours, skimming frequently. When the meat is tender, drain; strain and reserve the stock.

🔥 Finely chop the remaining carrot and onion, the bay leaf and the prosciutto. Heat the oil in a saucepan. Add chopped ingredients and oxtail and sauté over moderate heat until browned. Add salt and pepper and stir well. Add the wine, tomatoes, thyme, cloves and lemon peel and simmer for 30 minutes, adding reserved stock as required. Transfer to a serving dish and serve hot.

Serves 6

OXTAIL RAGOUT

STEAKS WITH TOMATO, GARLIC AND OREGANO SAUCE

Campania

BRACIOLE ALLA PIZZAIOLA
STEAKS WITH TOMATO, GARLIC AND OREGANO SAUCE

This sauce is called pizzaiola *because the beef is cooked like a pizza with oil, garlic, oregano and tomatoes.* Braciole *are very thin, wide slices of beef without bone.*

¼ cup (2 fl oz/60 ml) extra virgin olive oil
1 garlic clove, peeled
6 thin slices of beef, 5 oz (155 g) each
1 lb (500 g) tomatoes, peeled and coarsely
   chopped

salt and freshly ground pepper
1 tablespoon chopped fresh oregano
   (or 2 teaspoons dried oregano)

❧ Heat the oil with the garlic in a cast iron skillet over high heat. Add the meat and brown on both sides. Add the tomatoes, season with salt and pepper and bring to boil.
❧ Turn down the heat. Sprinkle the oregano over the meat and tomatoes, partially cover the pan and cook for 20 minutes more to reduce the sauce before serving.

Serves 6

AGNELLO AL FINOCCHIO

LAMB AND FENNEL

The Sardinians have special expertise in the breeding of sheep. Their lambs are particularly tender because they are slaughtered when very young, weighing no more than 20 lb (10 kg). Lamb is almost the only meat eaten on the island of Sardinia.

1 shoulder of lamb, about 3 lb (1.5 kg)
¼ cup (2 fl oz/60 ml) extra virgin olive oil
1 onion, chopped
salt and freshly ground pepper
1 lb (500 g) canned peeled tomatoes
1 lb (500 g) small wild fennel stalks, or
  2 fennel bulbs with leaves

🖘 Wash and dry the lamb and cut into pieces.
🖘 Heat the oil in a large skillet, add the onion and lamb and sauté over moderate heat until the lamb is browned. Add salt, pepper and tomatoes, cover and cook over low heat for 10 minutes.
🖘 Trim the fennel and cut into small pieces. Add to the lamb and cook uncovered until the meat is very tender, for about 1½ hours, adding a little water if necessary. Adjust the seasoning. Arrange the lamb in a dish and serve.

Serves 6

LAMB AND FENNEL (LEFT) AND GRILLED LAMB CHOPS SERVED WITH SLICED CUCUMBER, LEMON AND FENNEL (RIGHT, RECIPE PAGE 69)

Emilia-Romagna

ROLLÈ DI TACCHINO ALLA BOLOGNESE
STUFFED TURKEY ROLL

Stuffed meats are a common feature of the cooking of Emilia-Romagna. Sometimes a single large slice of turkey or veal is stuffed, sometimes small individual rolls called involtini *are served, and sometimes an entire* cotechino *(a large sausage made by filling a pork casing with ground pork and spices) is rolled into a slice of meat. In each case the filling is flavored with plenty of* parmigiano reggiano, *the Parmesan cheese from the district of Reggio-Emilia.*

2 eggs
½ cup (2 oz/60 g) freshly grated Parmesan
    cheese
salt and freshly ground pepper
3 tablespoons extra virgin olive oil
10 cups (10 oz/315 g) spinach, chopped
pinch of freshly grated nutmeg
1 slice turkey, about ⅜ in (1 cm) thick and
    about 1¼ lb (600 g)
1 tablespoon chopped fresh rosemary
3 oz (90 g) thinly sliced *pancetta* or rindless bacon
1 tablespoon unsalted butter
1 cup (8 fl oz/250 ml) dry white wine

Beat the eggs in a bowl with the cheese; season with salt and pepper. Heat 1 tablespoon of olive oil in a cast iron skillet and pour in the egg mixture. Cook the omelet on both sides.

Heat another tablespoon of oil in a large saucepan, add spinach and cook over low heat until wilted. Sprinkle with the nutmeg and add salt to taste. Arrange the omelet, spinach, rosemary and pancetta on top of the turkey. Roll up the meat and tie it securely, enclosing the filling completely.

Preheat an oven to 350°F (180°C). Heat the butter and the remaining oil in a large ovenproof skillet and brown the turkey roll on all sides over high heat. Pour in half the wine and let it evaporate. Transfer the turkey to the oven for 1 hour.

Lift out the meat and keep warm. Pour the rest of the wine into the pan and bring to boil, scraping up browned bits. Slice the meat and pour the pan juices over it before serving.

Serves 6

Lazio

COSTOLETTE D'AGNELLO A SCOTTADITO
GRILLED LAMB CHOPS

The Romans love these lamb chops, which are quite small and cut ⅜ in (1 cm) thick. They are cooked either on a grill or in a very hot cast iron skillet that has been lightly sprinkled with table salt.

1⅔ lb (815 g) lamb chops (cutlets) with bone
juice of 1 lemon
¼ cup (2 fl oz/60 ml) extra virgin olive oil
salt and freshly ground pepper

Place the chops on a plate and squeeze half the lemon juice over them. Add the oil, salt and pepper. Let the chops marinate for about 1 hour, turning from time to time.

Pat the meat dry and cook for just a few minutes on each side on a very hot grill or in a cast iron skillet that has been lightly sprinkled with salt. Arrange the chops on a serving plate, season with salt and pepper and squeeze the rest of the lemon juice over them. Serve at once.

Serves 6   *Photograph page 67*

about 10 bay leaves
2 onions, chopped
salt and freshly ground pepper
1 cup (8 fl oz//250 ml) dry white wine

🜚 Heat the oil in a saucepan just large enough to hold the meat. Add pork and brown over moderate heat for about 10 minutes. Add juniper berries, cloves, bay leaves, onions, salt and pepper.

🜚 Lower the heat and cook the meat until very tender, about 1½ hours, adding ½ cup (4 fl oz/125 ml) wine a little at a time.

🜚 Slice the meat and arrange on a serving dish. Pour the remaining wine into the pan and bring to boil, scraping up browned bits. Put this sauce through a sieve and pour it over the meat. Serve immediately.

Serves 6

PORK WITH BAY LEAVES

Basilicata

MAIALE ALL'ALLORO
PORK WITH BAY LEAVES

In Basilicata, where the soil is rather unproductive, the farmers breed pigs, lambs, poultry and rabbits. Small villages cling to the mountaintops, rugged cliffs line the coast and the sea is deep and stunningly beautiful. Its most famous tourist city is Maratea.

2 tablespoons extra virgin olive oil
1 loin of pork, about 2 lb (1 kg)
1 tablespoon juniper berries, finely
  chopped
2 whole cloves

Emilia-Romagna

CAPPONE BOLLITO IN SALSA VERDE
BOILED CAPON WITH GREEN SAUCE

Boiled capon is a northern Italian dish that is traditionally eaten at Christmas. It may be accompanied by green sauce or mostarda di Cremona, *or simply served with extra virgin olive oil mixed with a little lemon juice, salt and pepper.*

1 capon (or 1 large chicken), about 5 lb
  (2.5 kg), cleaned
1 carrot, cut into several pieces
1 celery stalk, cut into several pieces
1 small onion, stuck with 1 clove

several parsley sprigs tied into a small bunch, plus ½ cup (½ oz/15 g) loose parsley

1 tablespoon fresh breadcrumbs, soaked in red wine vinegar and squeezed dry

1 garlic clove, minced

2 anchovy fillets, mashed

½ cup (4 fl oz/125 ml) extra virgin olive oil

1 tablespoon drained capers

1 hard-boiled (hard-cooked) egg, chopped

salt and freshly ground pepper

Place the capon in a saucepan with cold salted water to cover; bring to a boil. Add the carrot, celery, onion and bunch of parsley and poach over low heat for 2 hours.

Meanwhile, mince the rest of the parsley. Mix with breadcrumbs, garlic and anchovies. Add the oil, capers and egg; season with salt and pepper.

Lift the capon out of the cooking stock and arrange on a platter. Pour the sauce into a sauceboat and serve separately.

Serves 6

BOILED CAPON WITH GREEN SAUCE SERVED WITH BOILED POTATOES

FEGATELLI DI MAIALE AL FINOCCHIO
PORK LIVER WITH FENNEL

This is a specialty of Chianti and the area around Siena, where fennel grows wild in every field and where pigs are allowed to roam free to feed on acorns from the oaks that abound there.

1 piece caul fat (see glossary)
1⅔ lb (800 g) pork liver
6 garlic cloves
salt and freshly ground pepper
3 tablespoons fennel seeds
6 thick slices firm, coarse-textured bread
24 bay leaves
¼ cup (2 fl oz/60 ml) extra virgin olive oil

Soak the caul fat for about 1 hour in a bowl of lukewarm water to soften it. Drain well and pat dry with a kitchen towel. Lay the caul fat on a table or board. Divide it and the liver into 12 pieces.

Mash the garlic with a little salt, plenty of pepper and fennel seeds; coat the liver with this mixture. As each piece is coated, wrap it in a piece of the caul fat. Cut the bread as neatly as possible into 18 equal pieces.

Preheat an oven to 350°F (180°C). Thread the ingredients onto 6 metal skewers, beginning with a piece of bread, then a bay leaf, a piece of liver, another bay leaf, bread, bay leaf, liver, bay leaf, and finally another piece of bread. Line the skewers up on a shallow baking dish with each end of the skewers resting on the sides of the dish so that the meat does not touch the bottom. Brush with a little olive oil, paying special attention to the bread. Bake until liver is cooked through, about 40 minutes, turning often and basting frequently with the remaining oil. Transfer the skewers to a platter and serve.

Serves 6   *Photograph page 50*

COTECHINO CON LENTICCHIE
PORK SAUSAGE WITH LENTILS

A cotechino *is a large pork sausage made by stuffing a pork casing with a mixture of ground meat and fat. Before it is cooked it must be pricked all over with a fork; it is then wrapped in a fine cloth and tied securely.*

2½ cups (18 oz/560 g) lentils
3 oz (90 g) *pancetta* or rindless bacon, finely chopped
3 bay leaves
1 *cotechino* Italian pork sausage, about 2 lb (1 kg)
salt and freshly ground pepper
1 cup (8 fl oz/250 ml) water

Soak the lentils in cold water to cover for 12 hours. Discard any that float to the surface, and drain the rest.

Cook the bacon in a large saucepan over medium-high heat until crisp. Add the lentils and bay leaves, season with salt and pepper and pour in 1 cup water. Cover and cook until all is absorbed, about 30 minutes. Discard the bay leaves. Wrap the sausage in a fine cloth and simmer separately in water to cover for 1½ hours. Drain, remove the cloth, slice and place on a platter. Arrange the warmed lentils around sausage and serve.

Serves 6   *Photograph page 50*

ROAST CHICKEN

Puglia

POLLO ARROSTO

ROAST CHICKEN

Chickens in Italy are usually lean and rather small. Country housewives often raise them for family consumption, and sometimes they sell them. Chickens bred in this way, known as farmyard or free-range chickens, are the tastiest.

1 chicken, about 3 lb (1.5 kg)
1 lemon
salt and freshly ground pepper
1 fresh rosemary sprig
2 tablespoons extra virgin olive oil
½ cup (4 fl oz/125 ml) dry white wine

Clean the chicken; wash and dry it well. Wash the lemon but do not peel it: place it inside the chicken. Salt and pepper the inside of the chicken and sew up the cavity with thread.

Preheat an oven to 350°F (180°C). Chop the rosemary leaves, add a little salt and rub the chicken all over with this mixture. Heat the oil in a shallow ovenproof skillet, add the chicken and brown on all sides over moderate heat. Transfer it to the oven and roast for 1½ hours.

Take out the stitching and discard the lemon. Place the chicken onto a serving dish and keep warm. Pour the wine into the skillet and boil for a few minutes, scraping up browned bits. Pour this sauce into a gravy boat and serve separately.

Serves 4

PHEASANT WITH OLIVES

FAGIANO ALLE OLIVE
PHEASANT WITH OLIVES

Pheasant is cooked during the hunting season—from September to March. The flesh of the newly killed pheasant is rather leathery, so it must be hung to age for five or six days before it is cleaned. Before cooking, the entrails and feathers must be removed.

2 oz (60 g) sliced *pancetta* or rindless bacon
1 pheasant, dressed
1 cup (4 oz/125 g) pitted black olives
1 tablespoon fennel seeds
1 tablespoon unsalted butter
2 tablespoons extra virgin olive oil
salt and freshly ground pepper
1 tablespoon juniper berries, crushed
½ cup (4 fl oz/125 ml) dry white wine
¼ cup (2 fl oz/60 ml) meat or chicken broth
  (stock)

Preheat an oven to 375°F (190°C). Wrap the bacon slices around the breast of the pheasant and tie it securely. Stuff the bird with the olives and fennel seeds, and sew up the cavity.

Heat the butter and oil in an ovenproof skillet over medium heat and brown the pheasant slowly for 20 minutes. Season with salt, pepper and juniper berries. Add the wine and let it evaporate. Add the broth and roast for 1 hour, basting often with the pan juices.

Cut the bird into serving pieces and arrange the stuffing around it. Place pan over medium heat and use a little water to help scrape up browned bits from the bottom. Pour this sauce through a sieve over the bird and serve.

Serves 6

FLORENTINE MEAT AND VEGETABLE FRITTERS

bowl of water with lemon juice added to prevent them from turning brown.

🔊 Open the zucchini flowers and remove the pistils. Beat the eggs well in a shallow bowl with salt and pepper. Dry all the vegetables well. Dredge all the meat, vegetables and zucchini flowers in flour, then coat with egg.

🔊 Fry a few pieces at a time until crisp and golden; do not let pieces stick to bottom of pan. Drain on paper towels and serve piping hot.

Serves 6

Toscana

FRITTO MISTO ALLA FIORENTINA
FLORENTINE MEAT AND VEGETABLE FRITTERS

The Florentine "mixed fry" consists of chicken, rabbit and vegetables such as artichokes, zucchini and zucchini flowers. Unlike the Piedmontese version, this one is cooked in extra virgin olive oil, which makes it crisper.

½ chicken
½ rabbit
2 small zucchini (courgettes)
2 globe artichokes, leaf tips trimmed
juice of 1 lemon
6 zucchini (courgette) flowers, optional
2 eggs
salt and freshly ground pepper
¾ cup (4 oz/125 g) all-purpose (plain) flour
extra virgin olive oil for frying

🔊 Cut the chicken and rabbit into smallish pieces, the zucchini into short strips and the artichokes into small wedges. Remove chokes from artichokes. Place the artichokes in a

Veneto

PICCIONI RIPIENI
STUFFED PIGEONS

Pigeons are often served on their own as a main dish accompanied by a risotto *flavored with either fresh mushrooms or peas. In this case the bread is eliminated.*

3 pigeons (Cornish hens or squab)
3 oz (90 g) cooked ham, thinly sliced and chopped
½ cup breadcrumbs, without crusts, soaked in milk and squeezed dry
1 egg
1 tablespoon chopped onion
2 oz (60 g) pork fat, chopped
6 fresh sage leaves, chopped
1 tablespoon juniper berries, crushed
salt and freshly ground pepper
3 fresh rosemary sprigs
2 tablespoons extra virgin olive oil
1 tablespoon unsalted butter
1 cup (8 fl oz/250 ml) dry white wine
6 slices firm, coarse-textured bread

Clean the pigeons and take out the livers. Mix the ham, bread, egg, onion, pork fat, sage, juniper berries, salt and pepper. Stuff the pigeons with this mixture, adding a whole sprig of rosemary to each.

Grease a shallow pan with the oil and butter and brown the pigeons over moderate heat. Pour in a little wine, lower the heat and cook, covered, for 1 hour, adding the remaining wine a little at a time.

Meanwhile, toast the slices of bread until golden. Arrange on a serving dish. Cut the pigeons in half and place a half on each slice of bread. Pour the cooking juices over and serve.

Serves 6   *Photograph page 6*

Trentino – Alto Adige

ANITRA ALLE PRUGNE
DUCK WITH PRUNES

The cooking of the Trentino region shows considerable Austrian influence, and often meat—especially duck and game such as roebuck, deer and hare—is cooked with prunes, cranberries or red currants, or accompanied by stewed chestnuts.

7 oz (220 g) dried prunes
1 duck, about 3 lb (1.5 kg)
salt and freshly ground pepper
1 lemon, sliced
½ cup (4 fl oz/125 ml) dry white wine
stewed chestnuts as an accompaniment

Soak the prunes in lukewarm water to cover. When they are nicely swollen, drain and pit them.

Preheat an oven to 350°F (180°C). Wash the duck and discard the heart and liver; pat dry. Rub inside and out with salt and pepper. Stuff the duck with the prunes and lemon slices. Sew up the cavity and place in a buttered flameproof baking dish.

Roast for 2 hours or until joints rotate easily, basting the duck frequently with the fat that melts in the baking dish. Lift out the duck, cut it into serving pieces and arrange on a platter. Remove prunes from cavity and keep warm; discard lemon.

Discard the fat from the baking dish and pour in the wine, scraping up browned bits and stirring over moderate heat until slightly thickened. Pour sauce over the duck, arrange the prunes and chestnuts around it and serve.

Serves 6

DUCK WITH PRUNES

CONIGLIO ALLA BARESE
BARI-STYLE RABBIT

Raisins and pine nuts feature in many traditional meat and pasta dishes of southern Italy. The pine nuts are found in the ripe cones that fall from umbrella pines, protected by a husk that must be broken with care so that the nuts may be extracted whole.

½ cup (3 oz/90 g) golden raisins (sultanas)
1 rabbit, about 4 lb (2 kg)
¼ cup (2 fl oz/60 ml) extra virgin olive oil
2 tablespoons sugar
1 tablespoon all-purpose (plain) flour
½ cup (4 fl oz/125 ml) white wine vinegar
salt and freshly ground pepper
1 tablespoon chopped fresh thyme
2 bay leaves
1 fresh rosemary sprig
1 cup (8 fl oz/250 ml) meat broth (stock)
½ cup (3 oz/90 g) pine nuts

✷ Soak the raisins in lukewarm water to cover until needed. Cut the rabbit into pieces: 2 forelegs; 2 hind legs; the saddle cut in two, kidneys attached; and rib cage split in two; wash and dry well. Heat the oil in a large skillet, add the rabbit pieces and brown over moderate heat.

✷ Pour off excess fat from the pan. Sprinkle in the sugar, flour, vinegar, salt and pepper and simmer until the liquid is completely absorbed. Add the thyme, bay leaves and rosemary.

✷ Pour in the broth and add the drained raisins. Cover and simmer for 40 minutes. Discard the rosemary, scatter the pine nuts over and serve.

Serves 6

CONIGLIO ALL'ANCONETANA
STUFFED RABBIT

Stuffed rabbit is a specialty of Ancona. Sometimes the filling is enriched with chopped black olives and a couple of chopped anchovy fillets.

1 rabbit, about 2½ lb (1.25 kg)
3 garlic cloves
3 oz (90 g) prosciutto
3 oz (90 g) firm, coarse-textured bread
½ cup (4 fl oz/125 ml) milk
salt and freshly ground pepper
pinch of ground nutmeg
½ cup chopped fennel tops
¼ cup (2 fl oz/60 ml) extra virgin olive oil
grated rind of 1 lemon

✷ Wash the rabbit thoroughly under running water. Reserve the heart and liver. Finely chop together the rabbit heart and liver, 1 of the garlic cloves and half of the prosciutto. Crumble the bread into a small bowl. Add the milk, a pinch each of salt and pepper and the nutmeg and let soak.

✷ Add 2 garlic cloves to a small amount of lightly salted water in a large saucepan. Add the fennel, cover and steam for 15 minutes. Discard the garlic cloves. Drain the fennel and squeeze dry, reserving the cooking liquid; chop finely with the remaining prosciutto.

✷ Place the fennel and prosciutto in a saucepan with half the oil and the lemon rind and cook over low heat for 10 minutes to blend the flavors.

✷ Squeeze the bread dry. Remove fennel mixture from the heat and add the bread and

STUFFED RABBIT (TOP) AND BARI-STYLE RABBIT SERVED WITH SPAGHETTI (BOTTOM)

the rabbit heart and liver. Stir until smooth. Preheat an oven to 350°F (180°C). Fill the cavity of the rabbit with the prepared stuffing and sew up the opening. Place in an oiled baking dish and season with salt and pepper. Bake 1½ hours, basting occasionally with the fennel cooking liquid.

When the rabbit is almost cooked, turn up the heat to 425°F (220°C) to brown it for 5 minutes. The rabbit is cooked if the juices run clear when pierced with a skewer. Cut the rabbit into pieces and serve.

Serves 6

LE VERDURE

WHEN WAS the vegetable garden first heard of in Italy? It is impossible to say exactly, but certainly the ancient Latin authors were already writing about it with some technical expertise. As far back as that time doctors and farmers had a complementary involvement in the *hortus,* one being concerned with health, the other with nourishment, and both beginning with the same raw materials.

The vegetable garden in Roman dwellings was within the house; limited in size, it produced vegetables, fruit and herbs. From the fall of the Roman Empire up to the early Middle Ages there was a distinct drop in the quality of vegetables grown, and many varieties survived only in the kitchen gardens of monasteries and castles. During the Renaissance, it became the custom to establish permanent vegetable gardens at the gates of the cities. But large fields of vegetable crops such as we are accustomed to seeing today are relatively recent, dating from the end of the eighteenth and the beginning of the nineteenth centuries. Today, Italy produces 200 million tons of vegetables a year, spread over about 50 different varieties. A considerable portion still comes from small family-run market gardens.

From a list given in *Tacuinum Sanitatis,* a late fifteenth-century work, it appears that many of the vegetables in use at that time were the same as those we use today: lettuce, with which the ancients suggested diners should *claudere coenas* (finish dinner) because it would do them good; cabbage; spinach, which it was recommended should be cooked without water so as not to lose the nutrients; celery; leeks; turnips, to be pickled; fennel; onions; asparagus; pumpkin; garlic; basil; parsley; chickpeas; eggplants (aubergines); and salads, the favorite food of young girls. With the discovery of new lands, the vegetable garden was enriched with potatoes, tomatoes, peppers (capsicums) and beans, as well as numerous varieties of fruits and cereals.

Vegetables must be shiny, bright in color and firm to the touch. They may be boiled, stewed or marinated. The proper way to boil them is to use only a small amount of salted water—except for potatoes, which require a cold-water start—and to cook them uncovered so they do not lose their bright color. Remember not to cook vegetables for too long; they must always retain a certain firmness. Steaming is also an excellent way to keep in the flavor.

Stewed vegetables use oil or butter but no water, because the vegetables exude their own juices during cooking. For stewing it is preferable to use a terracotta pan with a lid, so the vegetables cook slowly and evenly and do not stick to the pan.

BROAD BEANS AND BACON (TOP, RECIPE PAGE 90), CELERY WITH MARROW SAUCE (BOTTOM LEFT, RECIPE PAGE 86) AND BAKED POTATOES AND MUSHROOMS (BOTTOM RIGHT, RECIPE PAGE 96)

ASPARAGUS WITH PARMESAN CHEESE

Emilia - Romagna

ASPARAGI ALLA PARMIGIANA

ASPARAGUS WITH PARMESAN CHEESE

The asparagus grown in Emilia-Romagna is a pale violet color. This method of preparing asparagus is characteristic of the north of Italy, in contrast to the plainer oil-and-lemon dressing used in Tuscany. The dish is often served with eggs fried in butter.

4 lb (2 kg) asparagus
¾ cup (3 oz/90 g) freshly grated Parmesan
　cheese
salt and freshly ground pepper
⅓ cup (3 oz/90 g) unsalted butter

In a tall, narrow saucepan, bring enough salted water to boil to reach just below the asparagus tips. Clean the asparagus, and tie it in bunches. Add to the saucepan, stems down, and cook just until crisp-tender. Drain and transfer to a serving dish.

Untie the asparagus and sprinkle the green tips with Parmesan, salt and pepper. Keep hot.

Meanwhile, heat the butter in a small saucepan until light brown. Pour it over the asparagus and serve.

Serves 6

Veneto

RADICCHIO ALLA PANCETTA

RADICCHIO WITH BACON

The radicchio from Castelfranco Veneto is round like a ball, with slightly wrinkled leaves that are variegated white and dark red. It is not as tender as the variety grown in Treviso, but it is easier to find and less expensive.

2 tablespoons extra virgin olive oil
3 oz (90 g) smoked *pancetta* or rindless bacon, cut into strips
1 onion, sliced

2 lb (1 kg) Castelfranco *radicchio* or Belgian endive
salt and freshly ground pepper

🍴 Heat the oil in a skillet over low heat. Add the *pancetta* and onion and sauté for 15 minutes, stirring frequently.

🍴 Trim the *radicchio* and discard the root. Cut into lengthwise wedges. Add to the skillet and season with salt and pepper. Cook over low heat, turning carefully, for 5 minutes. Transfer to a platter and serve.

Serves 6

RADICCHIO WITH BACON

GREEN BEANS WITH TOMATO AND BELL PEPPER SAUCE (LEFT) AND PEPPER AND TOMATO STEW (RIGHT, RECIPE PAGE 86)

FAGIOLINI ALLA PEPERONATA

GREEN BEANS WITH TOMATO AND BELL PEPPER SAUCE

In Sicily, the tomato reigns everywhere. It is added to meat, fish, pasta and other vegetables. The tomatoes of this region are particularly flavorful and have a very thin skin because they are left to ripen on the plant in the hot Sicilian sun and are picked only when ready to eat.

2 ripe tomatoes
2 yellow bell peppers (capsicums)
3 tablespoons extra virgin olive oil
1 onion, sliced
2 garlic cloves, chopped
1¼ lb (625 g) green beans
salt and freshly ground pepper
2 tablespoons chopped fresh oregano

Drop the tomatoes into a saucepan of boiling water for a few seconds, then peel and chop them. Halve and seed the peppers, then cut into strips.

Heat the oil in a skillet, add the onion and garlic and sauté until the onion is golden. Add the peppers and cook gently for 5 minutes. Add the tomatoes and cook over medium-low heat for 30 minutes.

Meanwhile, trim the beans and cook them for 2 minutes in a large pot of boiling salted water. Drain and add to the other vegetables. Season with salt and pepper and finish cooking for a few more minutes. Transfer to a serving plate, sprinkle with the oregano and serve.

Serves 6

SEDANO AL MIDOLLO
CELERY WITH MARROW SAUCE

Beef marrow is found in the bones of the cow's hooves. It is used in the preparation of many dishes, sometimes raw and sometimes previously boiled. Whether raw or cooked, it is easily extracted from the bones with slight pressure of the fingers.

1 carrot, sliced
½ onion, sliced
3 bunches celery
1 cup (8 fl oz/250 ml) meat broth
   (stock)
salt and freshly ground pepper
1 bay leaf
½ cup (4 fl oz/125 ml) Marsala
2 marrow bones, about 2 in (5 cm) long
1 teaspoon fresh lemon juice

Combine the carrot and onion in a large saucepan. Cut the celery into 2½-in (6-cm) lengths. Place on top of the carrot mixture and pour in broth. Season with salt, pepper and bay leaf. Cover and cook over low heat for 30 minutes. Add the Marsala and lower the heat as far as possible so that the contents of the saucepan are just kept hot.

Meanwhile, cover the bones with water in another saucepan. Bring to boil and cook over low heat for 15 minutes. Push the marrow out of the bones and chop it. Add to celery mixture with lemon juice and salt and pepper to taste. Simmer for another few minutes before serving.

Serves 6   *Photograph page 80*

PEPERONATA
PEPPER AND TOMATO STEW

Peperonata is an excellent accompaniment to meat or fish, and it can also be used as a sauce for spaghetti, rigatoni *or* penne. *Sometimes it is enriched with capers and anchovy fillets.*

3 ripe tomatoes
6 red and yellow bell peppers (capsicums)
¼ cup (2 fl oz/60 ml) extra virgin
   olive oil
1 onion, sliced
2 garlic cloves, chopped
salt
1 tablespoon chopped fresh oregano
a few fresh basil leaves

Plunge the tomatoes and peppers into boiling water for a few seconds; drain and peel them. Chop the tomatoes; seed and slice the peppers.

Heat the oil in a skillet over medium heat. Add the garlic and onion and sauté until translucent. Add the pepper slices and salt to taste, and cook for a few minutes. Add the tomatoes and oregano. Cover, reduce heat and cook slowly for 30 minutes, stirring from time to time. Add the basil and cook for a few minutes more to blend flavors. Transfer to a bowl and serve.

Serves 6   *Photograph pages 84–85*

CHESTNUTS AND BRUSSELS SPROUTS IN BUTTER

Trentino—Alto Adige

CASTAGNE E CAVOLINI AL BURRO
CHESTNUTS AND BRUSSELS SPROUTS IN BUTTER

Chestnuts are now relatively rare in Europe as a result of a disease that struck years ago, killing the trees. They are sold in the streets, cooked in their skins on a brazier set up on a special cart.

1¼ lb (615 g) chestnuts
2 tablespoons unsalted butter
1 celery stalk, cut into strips
10 oz (315 g) Brussels sprouts, quartered

½ cup (4 fl oz/125 ml) dry white wine
salt

☙ Preheat an oven to 350°F (180°C). Place the chestnuts on a baking sheet and bake for 10 minutes. Remove the shells and the inner skins. Place the chestnuts in a skillet with the butter, celery and sprouts and sauté over low heat for 5 minutes. Add the wine and salt and bring to boil. Cover and cook until sprouts are tender and all liquid is absorbed, about 10 minutes. Serve hot.

Serves 6

CAULIFLOWER WITH ANCHOVY SAUCE (TOP), SAUTÉED EGGPLANT (CENTER) AND ONIONS IN CHEESE SAUCE (BOTTOM)

Sicilia

CAVOLFIORE ALL'ACCIUGA

CAULIFLOWER WITH ANCHOVY SAUCE

The cauliflowers grown in Sicily are mainly of the green variety, which are sweeter than white ones.

1 cauliflower, about 3 lb (1.5 kg)
½ cup (4 fl oz/125 ml) extra virgin olive oil
3 garlic cloves, chopped
3 tablespoons dry breadcrumbs
6 anchovy fillets in oil, mashed
salt and freshly ground pepper

Trim the cauliflower, removing tough stems. Cook it stems down in boiling salted water until crisp-tender—the water must barely touch the tips so that they do not break; drain. Transfer to a serving dish and keep warm.

Heat the oil in a small skillet over medium-high heat. Add the garlic, breadcrumbs and anchovies and cook for 2 minutes, stirring constantly. Pour sauce over the cauliflower, season with salt and pepper and serve.

Serves 6

Liguria

MELANZANE AL FUNGHETTO
SAUTÉED EGGPLANT

The term al funghetto *means the vegetables are cooked very briefly, like mushrooms, and are flavored with garlic and parsley. The eggplants must be firm and not too large; choose oval rather than round ones because they have fewer seeds. If eggplants are not to be fried they should not be salted and left to drain, because they lose too much moisture and with it some of their flavor.*

1½ lb (750 g) eggplants (aubergines)
2 garlic cloves, chopped
¼ cup (2 fl oz/60 ml) extra virgin
  olive oil
salt
2 tablespoons chopped parsley

Cut the tops off the eggplants and cut them first into thick slices, then into cubes.

Fry the garlic gently in the oil in a large skillet. Add the eggplant and cook over moderate heat just until tender. Season with salt, sprinkle parsley over and serve.

Serves 6

Val d'Aosta

CIPOLLINE ALLA FONTINA
ONIONS IN CHEESE SAUCE

Cipolline *are round, flat and rather small onions, similar to pickling onions. They have a golden brown outer skin, which is removed. They are very sweet and have a long shelf life, and so are popular in winter. If they are unavailable, pearl (baby) onions may be used instead.*

2 lb (1 kg) small onions with skin on
½ tablespoon unsalted butter
1 tablespoon all-purpose (plain) flour
2 cups (16 fl oz/500 ml) milk
a pinch of powdered clove
salt and freshly ground pepper
3 oz (90 g) fontina or Gruyère cheese, thinly
  sliced
2 tablespoons chopped parsley

Bring a large saucepan of salted water to boil. Drop in the onions and boil gently for 20 minutes. Drain and peel them; keep warm.

Melt the butter in a wide skillet. Add the flour and mix well. Gradually pour in the milk, stirring constantly. Bring to boil and season with clove, salt and pepper. Add the cheese and allow it to melt, then stir in the parsley. Pour over onions and serve.

Serves 6

FAVE AL GUANCIALE
BROAD BEANS AND BACON

Broad beans are good only when they are very fresh and the pods are not too thick. They generally are ready for picking in May and June and do not last long. Guanciale is bacon made from a pig's cheek, but it may be replaced by pancetta or ordinary bacon.

3 oz (90 g) *guanciale, pancetta* or pork fat, chopped
1 small onion, sliced
6 lb (3 kg) broad beans, shelled
3 ripe tomatoes, peeled and chopped
salt and freshly ground pepper

Fry the meat slowly in a saucepan with the onion until onion is translucent. Add the beans and cook for a few minutes over low heat. Add the tomatoes, season to taste with salt and pepper, and continue cooking until all the liquid is absorbed. Transfer to a bowl and serve.

Serves 6   *Photograph page 80*

BIETOLINE ALL'ACCIUGATA
BEET GREENS WITH ANCHOVIES

Young beet greens can be used for this dish in the spring; substitute turnip greens during autumn and winter.

2 lb (1 kg) young beet greens or turnip greens

6 anchovy fillets in oil, mashed
6 garlic cloves, chopped
3 tablespoons extra virgin olive oil
salt and freshly ground pepper

Wash the beet greens several times; drain.

🍃 Place the beet greens in a large saucepan with a very small amount of salted water and cook over high heat for 2 minutes. Drain them and squeeze dry.

🍃 Mix the anchovy fillets and garlic. Heat the oil in a skillet over medium heat. Add the garlic mixture and fry until fragrant. Add the beet greens and season with salt and pepper.

🍃 Cook, covered, over low heat for 5 minutes. Serve at once.

Serves 6

Lombardia

ZUCCHINE AL BURRO VERSATO
ZUCCHINI WITH BLACK BUTTER SAUCE

This is a very popular way of serving boiled vegetables; it is suitable also for fennel, celery, cardoons and asparagus. The sage may be replaced by parsley leaves which, like the sage, should be fried in the butter.

12 small zucchini (courgettes)
3 tablespoons unsalted butter
¼ cup (¼ oz/7 g) fresh sage leaves
⅓ cup (1½ oz/40 g) freshly grated Parmesan cheese
salt and freshly ground pepper

🥢 Cook the zucchini whole in boiling salted water until tender but not mushy. Drain. Trim ends and cut the zucchini into pieces. Place them in a serving dish.

🥢 Meanwhile, heat the butter in a small saucepan with the sage until the butter is dark brown. Sprinkle the cheese over the zucchini. Add salt and pepper, pour the butter over and serve at once.

Serves 6   *Photograph pages 94–95*

Piemonte

PORRI AL VINO ROSSO
LEEKS IN RED WINE SAUCE

Leeks are mainly a winter vegetable. They are always full of soil, so it is a good idea to make cuts in the green part to make washing them easier. They are also excellent boiled and served with bechamel sauce and grated Parmesan cheese.

2 lb (1 kg) leeks
1 tablespoon unsalted butter
½ cup (4 fl oz/125 ml) red wine
1 beef bouillon (stock) cube

🥢 Remove the root and a little of the green part of the leeks. Quarter the green section lengthwise, cutting until you reach the white part. Wash well and shake off water.

🥢 Melt butter in a large skillet. Add the leeks, cover and sauté for a few minutes over low heat. Pour in the wine, add the lightly crumbled bouillon cube and cover the pan once more. Reduce the heat and braise leeks for 10 minutes. Lift them out of the pan with a slotted spoon, arrange on a serving plate and keep hot.

🥢 Boil the sauce over moderate heat until reduced to about ¼ cup (2 fl oz/60 ml). Pour it over the leeks and serve. Sprinkle with chopped parsley if desired.

Serves 4–6

Lombardia

COSTE ALLA BESCIAMELLA
BEET STALKS WITH BECHAMEL SAUCE

Bechamel is a white sauce widely used in the north of Italy over vegetables such as fennel, asparagus tips, celery and cardoons, and also on fish fillets and in pasta dishes. It can be flavored with dried porcini *mushrooms (or champignons), tomato paste or parsley.*

3 lb (1.5 kg) beet greens or Swiss chard (silverbeet)
2 tablespoons unsalted butter

LEEKS IN RED WINE SAUCE (TOP) AND BEET STALKS WITH BECHAMEL SAUCE (BOTTOM)

freshly ground pepper

2 tablespoons all-purpose (plain) flour

2 cups (16 fl oz/500 ml) milk, heated to boiling

grated nutmeg

¾ cup (3 oz/90 g) freshly grated Parmesan cheese

1 hard-boiled (hard-cooked) egg

salt

🔥 Remove the green leaves from the vegetables and reserve for another use. Cut the stalks into small pieces and blanch in a medium saucepan of boiling salted water for 2 minutes. Drain.

🔥 Melt 1 tablespoon butter in a skillet. Add a sprinkling of pepper. Stir in beet stalks and sauté them until just tender, about 5 minutes. Transfer to a baking dish.

🔥 To prepare the bechamel sauce: melt the remaining butter in a saucepan over low heat. Stir in the flour and cook for 1 minute. Add the boiling milk and mix well. Stir in the nutmeg, cheese, and salt and pepper to taste.

🔥 Preheat an oven to 400°F (200°C). Pour the sauce over the beet stalks and bake for 15 minutes. Sieve the hard-boiled egg over the top and bake for 5 minutes longer. Serve hot.

Serves 6

Liguria

FRICASSEA DI FUNGHI
MUSHROOMS IN LEMON SAUCE

Mushrooms grow in abundance on the Ligurian mountains and inland hills. A fricassee is a sauce based on egg and lemon juice, which is also good with meat and fish. Fricasseed vegetables such as mushrooms, zucchini (courgettes) and green beans are a specialty of Genoa.

2 lb (1 kg) fresh *porcini* (boletus) mushrooms
   or champignons
3 tablespoons unsalted butter
1 tablespoon chopped parsley
2 tablespoons chopped borage
salt and freshly ground pepper
1 tablespoon all-purpose (plain) flour
1 egg yolk
juice of 1 lemon

Wipe the mushrooms clean with a cloth but do not wash; trim and slice them. Sauté over high heat in 2 tablespoons butter for 5 minutes, stirring often. Scatter the parsley and borage over the mushrooms and season with salt and pepper. Remove from heat.

Melt the remaining butter and stir in the flour, egg yolk and lemon juice. Pour this sauce over the mushrooms. Stir well and place over low heat for a few minutes to thicken, but do not let sauce boil. Transfer to a serving dish and serve immediately.

Serves 6

ZUCCHINI WITH BLACK BUTTER SAUCE (LEFT, RECIPE PAGE 92) AND MUSHROOMS IN LEMON SAUCE (RIGHT)

TRAPANI-STYLE STUFFED MUSHROOMS

Puglia

FUNGHI ALLA TRAPANESE
TRAPANI-STYLE STUFFED MUSHROOMS

Mushrooms come into Apulia in abundance from the neighboring region of Calabria, which is far more mountainous. They are often cooked in ancient wood ovens once used for baking bread. The ovens were built in the trulli, *Apulia's characteristic cone-shaped dwellings.*

18 *porcini* (boletus) mushrooms, or *shiitake* mushrooms
1 onion, finely chopped
3 garlic cloves, finely chopped
6 anchovy fillets in oil, chopped
½ cup (4 fl oz/125 ml) extra virgin olive oil
salt and freshly ground pepper
1 egg, beaten
½ cup (1 oz/30 g) fresh breadcrumbs (crusts trimmed), soaked in milk and squeezed dry
½ cup (2 oz/60 g) freshly grated Parmesan cheese
¼ cup (⅓ oz/10 g) chopped parsley

⅓ cup (1½ oz/45 g) fine dry breadcrumbs
1 lemon

Wipe the mushrooms clean with a cloth but do not wash them. Cut off and chop the stalks. Combine the onion, garlic, anchovies and mushroom stalks in a skillet. Add half the oil and cook over medium-high heat, stirring, for 10 minutes. Remove from heat and season with salt and pepper.

Let the mixture cool, then add the egg, fresh breadcrumbs, Parmesan and parsley and stir with a wooden spoon until well blended.

Fill the mushroom caps with this mixture and sprinkle with the dry breadcrumbs.

Preheat an oven to 350°F (180°C). Brush a little oil on the bottom of a baking dish and arrange the mushrooms in it. Sprinkle with the remaining oil and bake until crumbs are golden, about 20 minutes. Squeeze a few drops of lemon juice over each and serve.

Serves 6

Liguria

TEGLIA DI PATATE E FUNGHI
BAKED POTATOES AND MUSHROOMS

Potatoes done this way are very simple to prepare and may also be served as a first course. When porcini *mushrooms are in season they are used fresh instead of dried, sautéed briefly in a little olive oil. Alternatively, the mushrooms may be replaced by fried slices of fresh artichoke.*

1 cup (3 oz/90 g) dried *porcini* (boletus) mushrooms or champignons

5 tablespoons extra virgin olive oil
2 onions, sliced
salt and freshly ground pepper
2 lb (1 kg) baking potatoes, peeled and
   thinly sliced
1 cup (4 oz/125 g) freshly grated Parmesan
   cheese
2 cups (16 fl oz/500 ml) milk

🌿 Soak the mushrooms in lukewarm water to cover for 1 hour. Drain them and sauté in 1 tablespoon oil over low heat for 5 minutes. Heat 2 tablespoons oil in a saucepan over low heat. Add onions, cover and cook until tender. Season with salt and pepper.

🌿 Preheat an oven to 350°F (180°C). Layer the potatoes, onions and mushrooms alternately in a large oiled baking dish; sprinkle each layer with Parmesan, salt and pepper. Pour the milk over the potatoes and bake for 1 hour, or until all the liquid is absorbed and a light golden crust has formed on top. Let rest for 5 minutes before serving.

Serves 6　　　　　　　*Photograph page 80*

Toscana

CARCIOFI ALLA NEPITELLA
ARTICHOKES WITH CALAMINT

Nepitella (satureia calamintha) is an herb that grows wild in Tuscany and many other areas of Italy during summer and autumn. It is used especially to add flavor to mushrooms and artichokes. The herb belongs to the mint family; if necessary, mint can be used as a substitute.

6 globe artichokes
juice of 1 lemon
3 tablespoons fresh calamint, catnip (catmint)
   or mint
salt and freshly ground pepper
3 tablespoons extra virgin olive oil

🌿 Clean the artichokes and remove the tough outer leaves and spiky tips. Drop them into water acidulated with the lemon juice so they do not darken. Peel the artichoke stalks and chop them with the calamint. Season with salt and pepper.

🌿 Open up the leaves slightly and fill the spaces with the calamint mixture. Drizzle the artichokes with 2 tablespoons oil. Stand the artichokes upright in an oiled skillet. Pour a few tablespoons of water over them and cover the pan. Cook over low heat until artichokes are tender, about 20 minutes, basting from time to time with the pan juices.

Serves 6

ARTICHOKES WITH CALAMINT

Calabria

PATATE ALLA SALSICCIA
POTATOES WITH SPICY ITALIAN SAUSAGE

Calabria is a barren region where vegetables are scarce; the people eat mostly dried legumes (pulses) such as beans and chickpeas. Legumes and potatoes are often combined with sausages, which in this area are highly spiced.

7 oz (220 g) spicy Italian sausage
3 tablespoons extra virgin olive oil
1 onion, chopped
6 large baking potatoes, peeled and sliced
salt and freshly ground pepper

Remove the skin from the sausage and break up the meat. Heat the oil in a large cast iron skillet. Add the meat, onion and potatoes and cook, covered, over low heat for 30 minutes. Uncover, increase the heat and sauté the potatoes until brown, stirring. Season with salt and pepper, and serve.

Serves 6

Abruzzi and Molise

PATATE ALLE OLIVE
POTATOES WITH OLIVES AND ANCHOVIES

In the cooking of central and southern Italy, flavors are strong and distinct, oil takes the place of butter, and often vegetables are combined with anchovies, capers, olives or tomatoes.

¼ cup (2 fl oz/60 ml) extra virgin olive oil
2 lb (1 kg) baking potatoes, peeled and cut
   into wedges

⅔ cup (3 oz/90 g) black olives, pitted and
   chopped
1 tablespoon drained capers, chopped
6 anchovy fillets in oil, chopped
salt and freshly ground pepper
1 tablespoon chopped parsley

Heat the oil in a cast iron skillet over medium-high heat. Add the potatoes; sprinkle with the olives, capers and anchovies. Season with salt and pepper.

Cover, reduce heat to medium and cook for 30 minutes, stirring gently from time to time but taking care not to break up the potatoes. Scatter the parsley over the potatoes and serve.

Serves 6

Piemonte

PATATE AL GRATIN
GRATIN OF POTATOES

Potatoes cooked in this way can also be served as an elegant first course. They may be flavored with dried porcini *mushrooms (or champignons) or with thinly sliced fontina or Gruyère cheese and chopped sautéed bacon or* pancetta.

2 lb (1 kg) baking potatoes, peeled and thinly
   sliced
1 tablespoon unsalted butter
2 cups (16 fl oz/500 ml) milk
1 cup (8 fl oz/250 ml) cream
1¾ cups (7 oz/220 g) freshly grated Parmesan
   cheese
grated nutmeg
salt and freshly ground pepper

POTATOES WITH SPICY ITALIAN SAUSAGE (TOP LEFT), POTATOES WITH OLIVES
AND ANCHOVIES (TOP RIGHT) AND GRATIN OF POTATOES (BOTTOM)

Preheat an oven to 350°F (180°C). Lay the potato slices slightly overlapping in a large baking dish greased with the butter.

Mix the milk, cream, half the Parmesan, the nutmeg, and salt and pepper. Pour this mixture over the potatoes and sprinkle with the remaining Parmesan. Bake until potatoes are tender, about 45 minutes, raising the oven temperature to 425°F (220°C) for the last 10 minutes to brown the crust. Serve hot.

Serves 6

I Dolci

THERE IS A SAYING that the dessert is the poetry of cooking, the lyrical point in any meal. Certainly it creates high expectations: "Is there dessert?" the guests wonder as the end of a dinner party approaches. "If you're good, I'll give you a piece of cake" is a common promise made by mothers, grandmothers and aunts to small children. Sweet foods can also generate considerable guilt feelings, provide consolation or be a prize earned.

Until relatively recently, sugar was a rare and precious substance. In the past, honey was used as a sweetener, while cane sugar, which came to Europe after the great discoveries of new lands, was, up to the eighteenth century, a luxury reserved for the tables of kings and princes. Then in 1747 a German chemist succeeded in extracting sugar from beets, and during the nineteenth century it began to be commercially produced and to form part of everybody's diet.

And so, Italian cakes and desserts must be divided into two eras: the ancient and the modern. The oldest sweets were created as variations on or improvements to bread and bread dough: *Pane di Natale* (Liguria), *Pan Pepato* (Tuscany), *Pandoro* (Veneto), *Pan Meino* (Lombardy), *Pan di Spagna* (Tuscany), *Panettone* (Lombardy), *Panforte* (Tuscany), and so on. Or they were variations beginning from the same basis as pasta, as in shortcrust pastry, Genoese pastry, almond pastry, marzipan, etc.

The ingredients in today's cakes and desserts are the same, with the addition of cocoa, liqueurs, and eggs in abundance. The principal difference is the introduction of highly sophisticated techniques, many of which were imported from nineteenth-century France, during the era of European "grand gastronomy" when pastry shops and coffeehouses abounded in the old capitals of the Belle Epoque.

But in Italian cooking the traditional homemade sweets and cakes continue to predominate. These are the classic family "plain but good" varieties, sweet dishes related to the farmer's calendar, local festivals and the work in the fields. *Castagnaccio,* a chestnut cake, *Pane dei Morti* (bread of the dead) and *Pane di Miglio,* a millet cake, were always baked in November. There were cakes or desserts for Christmas, *Carnevale,* Easter and harvest time. The end of every season was an occasion for finishing a meal with a special sweet dish.

Cake making requires, a certain amount of care and precision, and a good deal of imagination—precision in quantities and cooking times, which must be strictly followed, and imagination in the addition of a particular flavor combination, some personal touch to make the creation unique.

LEMON SORBET (TOP, RECIPE PAGE 109) AND
COFFEE WATER ICE (BOTTOM, RECIPE PAGE 111)

RICOTTA PIE

Campania

CROSTATA DI RICOTTA

RICOTTA PIE

Ricotta pie is a simplified version of pastiera. *It is also much richer because it contains chocolate. The pie may be finished off with toasted pine nuts or almonds, and a sprinkling of confectioners' (icing) sugar.*

2 cups (10 oz/315 g) all-purpose (plain) flour
6 egg yolks
⅓ cup (3 oz /90 g) unsalted butter
⅔ cup (5 oz/155 g) superfine (caster) sugar

2 tablespoons all-purpose (plain) flour
1 cup (8 fl oz/250 ml) milk
3 oz (90 g) semisweet (plain) chocolate
¼ cup (2 fl oz/60 ml) maraschino liqueur
8 oz (250 g) ricotta
pinch of ground cinnamon
grated rind of 1 lemon
1 egg white, beaten

To prepare the pastry: combine 2 cups flour, 3 egg yolks, butter and half the sugar and mix into a dough. Form into a ball, cover with plastic and let rest in the refrigerator while preparing the filling.

To prepare the filling: beat remaining 3 egg yolks with remaining sugar until light. Add 2 tablespoons flour and the milk and cook the mixture in a double boiler over simmering water until thick. Melt the chocolate with the maraschino liqueur. Stir into the egg mixture and let cool completely.

Put the ricotta through a sieve. Gradually stir in the custard, cinnamon and lemon rind. Mix well and set aside for 10 minutes.

Preheat an oven to 350°F (180°C). Butter and flour a 10-in (25-cm) pie pan. Roll out ¾ of the pastry dough in a circle and line the pan with it. Pour in the prepared filling and roll out the remaining dough into a circle to cover the top. Crimp edges together. Brush the top of the pie with a little beaten egg white and bake for about 40 minutes or until crust is golden brown. Let cool before serving.

Serves 6–8

Veneto

POLENTA DOLCE
SWEET POLENTA

There are two kinds of cornmeal to be found in the Veneto—yellow and white. Generally speaking, coarse-ground yellow cornmeal is more often used in Lombardy, but in the Veneto cooks tend to use the fine-ground variety, both yellow and white.

3 cups (24 fl oz/750 ml) milk
½ cup (4 oz/125 g) sugar
1 cup (5 oz/155 g) fine white cornmeal
1 egg
4 egg yolks

¼ cup (2 oz/60 g) unsalted butter, softened
grated rind of 2 lemons
2 tablespoons fine dry breadcrumbs
confectioners' (icing) sugar, optional

Bring the milk and sugar to boil in a saucepan. Gradually pour in the cornmeal, stirring constantly. Simmer until very thick, about 30 minutes. Let cool to lukewarm. Stir in the whole egg and yolks, butter and lemon rind.

Preheat an oven to 350°F (180°C). Butter a 9-in (23-cm) cake pan and sprinkle with the breadcrumbs. Spread the polenta in the pan and bake for 20 minutes. Turn out, sprinkle with confectioners' sugar and serve at room temperature.

Serves 6

SWEET POLENTA

PASTIERA

EASTER PIE

Pastiera is the traditional Neapolitan Easter pastry. Each family has its own recipe and discusses it at length with friends and neighbors, everybody tasting each other's and commenting on them all. This pastry is offered to guests for at least a week around Easter time (and that is how long the pastiera *will keep). It is traditionally left in the pan in which it is baked, never turned out.*

5 oz (155 g) whole wheat kernels (available in health food stores)
1⅔ cups (8 oz/250 g) all-purpose (plain) flour
½ cup (4 oz/125 g) unsalted butter
⅓ cup (3 oz/90 g) sugar
4 egg yolks
1⅓ cups (11 fl oz/310 ml) milk
grated rind of ½ orange
⅓ cup (3 oz/90 g) superfine (caster) sugar
1 teaspoon vanilla extract (essence)
8 oz (250 g) ricotta
2 tablespoons orange flower water
1 tablespoon chopped candied citron (see page 118)
1 tablespoon chopped candied orange peel
1 tablespoon chopped candied pumpkin
pinch of ground cinnamon
2 egg whites

Soak the wheat in cold water overnight.

Combine the flour, butter, ⅓ cup sugar and 1 egg yolk to make a dough; form into a ball. Let rest while preparing filling.

Drain the wheat and combine with the milk, orange rind and 1 tablespoon sugar and cook over low heat until mixture is creamy and porridgelike. Remove from heat and stir in vanilla.

In a bowl, combine the ricotta, 3 egg yolks, the remaining sugar, the wheat, orange flower water, candied fruit and cinnamon. Beat the

egg whites until stiff and fold into the mixture.
🦋 Preheat an oven to 350°F (180°C). Roll
out ¾ of the pastry dough and use it to line a
9-in (23-cm) pie pan. Fill with the ricotta
mixture. Roll out the remaining dough and
cut it into ⅜-in (1-cm) strips using a fluted
pastry wheel. Arrange the strips in a lattice

over the filling and crimp the edges. Bake
the *pastiera* for 1 hour or until the pastry is
golden brown.
🦋 Let cool, then let the pie rest for a few
hours before serving.

Serves 6–8

AMARETTI-STUFFED PEACHES

Piemonte

PESCHE RIPIENE AGLI AMARETTI

AMARETTI-STUFFED PEACHES

The most flavorful peaches are generally those with white flesh. For this recipe, however, the yellow-fleshed freestone ones are used.

½ cup (4 fl oz/125 ml) white wine
⅓ cup (3 oz/90 g) sugar
6 ripe peaches, peeled, halved and pitted
12 amaretti biscuits, crushed
1 egg yolk, beaten (see glossary)
3 tablespoons cream, whipped

🜂 Boil the wine and sugar for 5 minutes to form a syrup. Poach the peach halves in the syrup for 5 more minutes, then lift out with a slotted spoon and let cool.
🜂 Fold the amaretti crumbs and egg yolk into the cream. Fill the peach halves with the cream mixture. Arrange on a serving plate and pour the remaining wine syrup around them.

Serves 6

Toscana

TIRAMISÙ

TUSCAN TRIFLE

Tiramisù *("pick me up") is a modern version of a dessert first created in Siena, where it was called* zuppa del Duca *(the Duke's soup). From there it migrated to Florence, where it became very popular in the nineteenth century among the many English people who came to live in the city at that time. And so it was called* zuppa inglese— *English soup. Only recently, the same dessert with some variation—chiefly the substitution of rich mascarpone cheese for the original custard—has come to be called* tiramisù.

3 egg yolks
3 tablespoons superfine (caster) sugar
1⅓ cups (11 fl oz/330 ml) *vin santo,* Marsala or brandy
¼ cup (2 fl oz/60 ml) very strong espresso coffee
8 oz (250 g) mascarpone cheese, at room temperature
½ cup (4 fl oz/125 ml) cream
1 egg white (see glossary)
4 oz (125 g) *savoiardi* or ladyfingers (sponge fingers)

🜂 Make a *zabaglione* by beating the egg yolks and sugar in the top of a double boiler until ivory colored. Add ⅓ cup (3 fl oz/80 ml) liquor and whisk over gently simmering water until the mixture begins to thicken. Let cool.
🜂 Stir the coffee into the mascarpone. Whip the cream to soft peaks. Beat the egg white until stiff. Fold the egg white into the *zabaglione.* Dip the lady fingers into the

TUSCAN TRIFLE

remaining liquor and arrange in a single layer in the bottom of a 9-in (23-cm) bowl. Cover them with half the mascarpone, then half the *zabaglione* and half the cream. Repeat the layers, finishing with the cream. Refrigerate for several hours before serving.

Serves 6

NOODLE CAKE

DOLCE DI TAGLIERINI

NOODLE CAKE

This is a classic dish that may be made with the fine egg noodles known as taglierini *or with the very thin spaghetti called* capelli d'angelo *("angel's hair") or* vermicelli. *The cake is particularly good served hot or lukewarm; if allowed to cool completely it becomes heavy.*

½ cup (2 oz/60 g) raisins
6 eggs, separated
1 cup (7 oz/220 g) superfine (caster) sugar
8 oz (250 g) dry *taglierini* (or angel hair pasta or vermicelli)
8 oz (250 g) ricotta
1 teaspoon cinnamon

1 teaspoon ground cloves
pinch of salt
⅓ cup (2 oz/60 g) all-purpose (plain) flour
½ cup (2 oz/60 g) fine dry breadcrumbs
1 cup (8 oz/250 g) orange marmalade
1 cup (12 oz/350 g) honey

🕸 Soak the raisins in lukewarm water to cover for 30 minutes; drain. Beat the egg yolks with the sugar until very light and lemon colored.
🕸 Bring a large saucepan of salted water to boil. Add the pasta and boil for 2 minutes. Drain, then rinse briefly under cold water.
🕸 Beat the ricotta with the egg yolk mixture, cinnamon, cloves and salt. Stir in the flour a little at a time. Add the drained raisins and *taglierini*.

Preheat an oven to 400°F (200°C). Beat the egg whites to soft peaks and fold into ricotta mixture. Pour into a buttered 9-in (23-cm) cake pan lightly coated with breadcrumbs. Bake for 1 hour and 10 minutes. Purée the marmalade and honey in a food processor. Transfer to a saucepan and warm over low heat.

Unmold the cake onto a serving dish. While still warm, spread the surface with some of the marmalade sauce. Pour the remaining sauce into a pitcher and serve separately.

Serves 6–8

Sicilia

SORBETTO AL LIMONE
LEMON SORBET

Lemon sorbet is usually served halfway through the meal because it is an excellent digestive. Sicily is famous for its wonderfully fragrant lemons, certainly the best in the world. Lemon orchards are now replacing most of the orange orchards.

1 cup (8 fl oz/250 ml) water
1 cup (8 oz/250 g) sugar
3 cups (24 fl oz/750 ml) fresh lemon juice
1 egg white (see glossary)

Boil the water with the sugar for 5 minutes. Stir in the lemon juice and let cool, then place in the freezer until hard.

About a half hour before serving time, place sorbet in blender with the egg white and blend until it resembles snow. Return to the freezer for 30 minutes, then serve.

Serves 6 *Photograph page 100*

Veneto

ZABAIONE CON LE FRAGOLE
ZABAGLIONE WITH STRAWBERRIES

Zabaglione is an old Venetian dessert that can be varied in infinite ways. The classic version is made with Marsala, but vin santo, *white wine and other dessert wines are equally suitable.*

6 egg yolks
6 half-eggshells of superfine (caster) sugar
6 half-eggshells of Marsala
1 egg white (see glossary)
2½ cups (10 oz/310 g) small strawberries

In the top of a double boiler, whisk the egg yolks with the sugar until frothy. Stir in the Marsala. Place over gently simmering water and whisk until mixture is very thick and has doubled in volume. Remove from heat and, while beating, let cool completely. Beat the egg white until stiff and fold into the *zabaglione*.

Transfer the *zabaglione* to a dish, arrange the strawberries around it and serve warm.

Serves 6

ZABAGLIONE WITH STRAWBERRIES

Campania

GRANITA DI CAFFÈ
COFFEE WATER ICE

There isn't a coffee bar in Campania that does not offer granita di caffè in the summer months— sometimes with a dollop of whipped cream on top. In the more elegant bars the coffee is often flavored with a little cocoa.

4 oz (125 g) superfine (caster) sugar
2 tablespoons water
6 cups (48 fl oz/1.5 l) very strong espresso coffee
2 teaspoons unsweetened cocoa powder

⁂ Combine the sugar and water in a saucepan and heat until sugar is dissolved, then boil the syrup for several minutes.

⁂ Pour the coffee into the syrup, dissolve the cocoa in it and remove from heat. Let cool completely.

⁂ Pour the mixture into a bowl and freeze until solid, then transfer to a blender and blend for a few seconds until slushy. Spoon into 6 glasses and serve immediately.

Serves 6   *Photograph page 100*

RICE CAKES

Lazio

TORTINI DI RISO
RICE CAKES

These little cakes are often served in cafés with a cappuccino. To serve as dessert, spoon a fresh fruit purée over them.

¼ cup (1 oz/30 g) raisins
1 cup (6 oz/185 g) Arborio rice
2 cups (16 fl oz/500 ml) milk
½ cup (4 oz/125 g) sugar
grated rind of ½ lemon
pinch of ground cinnamon
½ cup (4 oz/125 g) unsalted butter
4 egg yolks
1 egg white
confectioners' (icing) sugar

⁂ Soak the raisins in water to cover until needed. Boil the rice in 4 cups (32 fl oz/1 l) boiling water for 5 minutes; drain. Bring milk and sugar to a boil, add rice, lemon rind and cinnamon. Cook over low heat until rice has absorbed all the milk, stirring constantly. Stir in butter, drained raisins and egg yolks and let cool. Whip the egg white until stiff and fold into the rice.

⁂ Preheat an oven to 350°F (180°C). Pour mixture into 6 buttered individual molds and bake for 45 minutes, or until a knife inserted in the center comes out clean.

⁂ Unmold puddings onto individual plates, sprinkle with sifted confectioners' sugar and serve.

Serves 6

APPLE STRUDEL

Trentino - Alto Adige

STRUDEL DI MELE
APPLE STRUDEL

Apple strudel is made with filo pastry, which is as thin as a veil and rather difficult to roll out by hand. It is possible to use puff pastry instead, but then the strudel becomes extremely rich. It is important that the apples are the mealy kind.

1⅔ cups (8 oz/250 g) all-purpose (plain) flour
1 egg
1 tablespoon sugar
pinch of salt
4–5 tablespoons (2½ oz/75 g) unsalted butter, melted

2 lb (1 kg) baking (cooking) apples, peeled, cored and sliced
½ teaspoon ground cinnamon
¼ cup (1½ oz/45 g) blanched slivered almonds
¼ cup (1 oz/30 g) golden raisins (sultanas), soaked and drained
grated rind of 1 orange
½ cup (4 oz/125 g) apple jelly (jam)
3 tablespoons confectioners' (icing) sugar

To make the pastry, heap the flour on a board and make a well in the center. Mix in the egg, sugar and salt. Add 3 tablespoons melted butter and enough water to form a smooth dough.

Cover with a heated bowl and let dough rest for 20 minutes. Then work it again, slapping it down on the board to make it more elastic. Gather dough up into a ball.

Roll dough out on a floured cloth with a floured rolling pin, making it as thin as possible. Brush the sheet with remaining melted butter. Spread evenly with apples; scatter the cinnamon, almonds, raisins and orange rind on top. Spoon the jelly over and sprinkle with 2 tablespoons powdered sugar.

Preheat an oven to 350°F (180°C). Carefully roll up the strudel, removing the cloth as you go, and flatten at each end so that the filling will not come out during baking. Butter a large baking sheet and slide the strudel onto it. Bake until golden brown, about 1 hour. Transfer the strudel to a plate, sift the remaining powdered sugar over it and serve.

Serves 6

Piemonte

GELATO DI CAFFÉ CON GLI AMARETTI

COFFEE ICE CREAM WITH AMARETTI BISCUITS

Italian coffee is roasted much darker than the coffee in other countries and is also more highly concentrated; that is the secret of its excellence.

4 egg yolks

½ cup (4 oz/125 g) superfine (caster) sugar

1 cup (8 fl oz/250 ml) strong espresso coffee

1 cup (8 fl oz/250 ml) cream

2 egg whites (see glossary)

12 amaretti biscuits, crushed

Beat the egg yolks with the sugar in the top of a double boiler until thick and lemon colored. Add the coffee and, stirring constantly, cook gently over simmering water until the mixture is thick. Let cool to room temperature.

Whip the cream until it stands in soft peaks. Beat the egg whites until stiff but not dry. Fold half the amaretti crumbs, the cream and the beaten egg whites into the cooled custard. Churn in an ice cream maker until frozen.

Divide ice cream among 6 serving dishes, or freeze until serving time. Sprinkle with the remaining amaretti crumbs and serve.

Serves 6

COFFEE ICE CREAM WITH AMARETTI BISCUITS

MOLDED RICE PUDDING

BUDINO DI RISO

MOLDED RICE PUDDING

This rice pudding may be enriched with soaked raisins and diced candied peel or citron.

1 cup (6 oz/185 g) Arborio rice

3 cups (24 fl oz/750 ml) milk

4 eggs, separated

½ cup (4 oz/125 g) plus 2 tablespoons superfine (caster) sugar

6 oz (185 g) semisweet (plain) chocolate

⅓ cup (3 oz/90 g) unsalted butter

½ cup (4 oz/125 g) red currant jelly

¼ cup (2 fl oz/60 ml) *vin santo* or sweet white wine

Bring a saucepan of salted water to boil. Add rice and cook 5 minutes. Drain. Return rice to saucepan, add milk and cook over low heat until all liquid is absorbed.

Beat the egg yolks with ½ cup sugar until light. Melt the chocolate and butter together in a heatproof bowl set over simmering water. Beat the egg whites to stiff peaks, gradually adding 2 tablespoons sugar.

Preheat an oven to 400°F (200°C). Combine rice, yolks, chocolate mixture and whites and fold gently to blend well. Turn into a buttered 9-in (23-cm) mold. Place mold in a larger pan; add boiling water to the pan to come halfway up sides of mold. Bake for 1 hour. Remove mold from water bath, reduce oven temperature to 325°F (160°C) and bake the pudding for 10 minutes longer.

Unmold onto a platter. Stir jelly and *vin santo* together over very low heat until jelly dissolves. Drizzle over pudding and serve.

Serves 6

Umbria

ROCCIATE

FRUIT AND NUT COOKIES

Like many Italian cookies, these very traditional ones are made more often than not for times of celebration. They are perfect for offering to visitors with a glass of sweet wine.

½ cup (3 oz/90 g) dried prunes
½ cup (3 oz/90 g) raisins
½ cup (3 oz/90 g) dried figs, stemmed and sliced
2 apples, peeled, cored and sliced
¼ cup (1¼ oz/40 g) hazelnuts, coarsely chopped
¼ cup (1¼ oz/40 g) almonds, coarsely chopped
¼ cup (1 oz/30 g) walnuts, coarsely chopped
¼ cup (1¼ oz/40 g) pine nuts
¼ cup (2 fl oz/60 ml) Marsala
⅓ cup (3 fl oz/80 ml) extra virgin olive oil
⅔ cup (5 oz/155 g) superfine (caster) sugar
1⅓ cups (7 oz/220 g) all-purpose (plain) flour
pinch of salt
confectioners' (icing) sugar

Soak the prunes and raisins in lukewarm water for 30 minutes; drain. Pit the prunes.

Mix the fruit and nuts in a bowl. Add the Marsala, 1 tablespoon oil and half the sugar. Sift the flour and salt together. Mix in the remaining oil and sugar and enough water to make a soft dough. Form into a ball and let rest, covered, for 30 minutes.

Divide the dough into 12 parts. Roll out each piece into a very thin square. Spread some of the fruit mixture on each square of dough, dividing it evenly.

Preheat an oven to 350°F (180°C). Roll the squares up into cylinders and place on a lightly greased baking sheet. Bake until golden, about 30 minutes. Sprinkle with sifted confectioners' sugar and serve.

Serves 6

FRUIT AND NUT COOKIES

Toscana

ZUCCOTTO

ALMOND AND CHOCOLATE CAKE

When zuccotto *is turned out, its domed surface is decorated in brown and white wedges of cocoa and confectioners' (icing) sugar. The base of the* zuccotto *is usually sponge cake, but* savoiardi *(crisp lady-fingers or sponge finger biscuits) may also be used.*

7 oz (220 g) semisweet (plain) chocolate
2 cups (16 fl oz/500 ml) cream
¾ cup (3 oz/90 g) plus 1 tablespoon
　confectioners' (icing) sugar
⅔ cup (3 oz/90 g) blanched toasted hazelnuts,
　chopped
½ cup (3 oz/(90 g) blanched toasted almonds,
　chopped
5 oz (155 g) sponge cake, cut into strips
¼ cup (2 fl oz/60 ml) maraschino
　liqueur
1 tablespoon unsweetened cocoa powder

Chop half the chocolate. Melt the other half over simmering water in a double boiler; let it cool to room temperature, stirring occasionally.

Whip the cream with the sugar. Fold half of it into the melted chocolate, adding the hazelnuts; fold the other half into the chopped chocolate, adding the almonds.

Line a hemispherical 7-in (18-cm) bowl with waxed paper, then with the sponge cake. Brush the cake with the maraschino liqueur. Spread the almond mixture in an even layer over the cake, then fill the center with the hazelnut mixture. Smooth the surface and cover with waxed paper. Chill for several hours.

Unmold the *zuccotto* onto a serving plate. Cut wedges from a circular piece of paper and hold over the cake; sift the remaining powdered sugar onto the cake to form white wedges. Cover the white wedges with the paper and sift the cocoa onto the alternate wedges. Serve at once.

Serves 6 *Photograph page 119*

Lombardia

PAN MEINO

CORNMEAL AND ELDERFLOWER CAKE

This dessert is especially popular in spring, when the elders are in bloom. It is also possible to find dried elderflowers in grocery stores. The cornmeal gives the cake extra lightness. Sometimes pan meino *is baked in individual pans instead of a single large cake pan.*

2 egg yolks
6 tablespoons (3 oz/90 g) superfine caster
　sugar
⅔ cup (3 oz/90 g) all-purpose (plain) flour
1½ cups (7 oz/220 g) fine cornmeal
pinch of salt
2 teaspoons baking powder
1 teaspoon elderflowers, chopped
⅓ cup plus 1 tablespoon (3½ oz/115 g)
　unsalted butter
½ cup (4 fl oz/125 ml) milk
1 cup (8 fl oz/250 ml) cream

Combine egg yolks with 4 tablespoons of sugar and beat until light and lemon colored.

Set aside 1 tablespoon flour. Mix remaining flour with the cornmeal, salt, baking powder

CORNMEAL AND ELDERFLOWER CAKE

and elderflowers. Melt ⅓ cup (3 oz/90 g) butter in a small saucepan and blend into the yolk mixture. Add the flour mixture alternately with the milk, beating until well blended after each addition.

Preheat oven to 350°F (180°C). Grease a 9-in (23-cm) cake pan with the remaining butter and sprinkle it with a little of the reserved sugar mixed with the reserved flour. Spread the dough in the pan, making it slightly higher in the center. Scatter the remaining sugar over the surface. Bake until top is golden, about 40 minutes. Let cake cool. Serve cold with cream.

Serves 6

Sicilia

CANNOLI

SICILIAN RICOTTA FRUIT PASTRIES

To make cannoli *you need little metal cylinders called* cannelli, *which are about ¾ in (2 cm) in diameter and 4 in (10 cm) long. If they are not available, wooden rods of the same size may be used.*

10 oz (315 g) ricotta
1 cup (8 oz/250 g) superfine (caster) sugar
½ cup (3 oz/90 g) mixed candied fruit peel
    (citron, orange peel, cherries), diced
    (see next recipe)
2 tablespoons shelled pistachio nuts, halved
2 cups (10 oz/315 g) all-purpose (plain) flour
¼ cup (2 fl oz/60 ml) dry white wine
2 tablespoons honey
pinch of salt
1 egg
1 egg white
oil for deep frying
additional egg white
1 tablespoon confectioners' (icing) sugar

🕲 Mix the ricotta with half the sugar, the candied fruit and the pistachios. Refrigerate.
🕲 Mound the flour on a board, make a well in the center and pour in the wine. Add the honey, the remaining sugar, the salt, whole egg and egg white and knead until you have a fairly stiff dough. Shape into a ball, wrap in plastic and refrigerate for 2 hours.
🕲 Roll dough out thinly and cut into 4-in (10-cm) squares. Wrap around the cylinders and press closed, using a little egg white to make them adhere. Heat the oil to 350°F (180°C). Fry the tubes until golden brown on all sides. Drain on paper towels and cool

completely. Slide the tubes of pastry off the cylinders before completely cold.
🕲 Spoon the ricotta mixture into a pastry bag fitted with a wide tip and fill the pastry tubes with it. Dust with powdered sugar and serve.

Serves 6

Sicilia

SCORZETTE CANDITE

CANDIED PEEL

Many Sicilian desserts are based on candied fruit, in particular, orange, citron and lemon peel. Other candied fruits may be prepared by the same method, especially cherries and pumpkin.

rind of 2 oranges
rind of 2 citrons, limes or grapefruit
rind of 2 lemons
sugar
3 tablespoons water
1 tablespoon almond oil, optional

🕲 Boil each rind separately in water to cover generously for 2 minutes. Drain and let dry. Cut rinds into thin strips; weigh them, and weigh an equal amount of sugar.
🕲 Place the sugar in a copper saucepan with the water and almond oil (if used) and place over moderate heat, stirring constantly. When the syrup becomes foamy, remove from heat and add the rinds, mixing until all pieces are thoroughly coated.
🕲 Lightly oil a work surface, tip the rind and syrup onto it and separate the pieces with a fork. Let cool, then transfer to a jar for storage.

Makes 1 cup

ALMOND AND CHOCOLATE CAKE (TOP, RECIPE PAGE 116)
AND SICILIAN RICOTTA AND FRUIT PASTRIES (BOTTOM)

GLOSSARY

Not all of the glossary entries appear in the recipes. Nonetheless, each offers an interesting piece of information about Italian food and cooking.

AGNOLOTTI: Filled egg pasta. Depending on region and shape, the same form of pasta can be known as *tortelli, tortellini* or *ravioli.*

AL FUNGHETTO: A method of cooking vegetables quickly over high heat with some kind of herb, so called after the manner of cooking *porcini* (boletus) mushrooms *(fungi).* The main vegetables cooked *al funghetto* are eggplants (aubergines) and zucchini.

AMARETTI: Crisp macaroons made with bitter almonds (*amaro* means bitter), which will keep for long periods. The best known are the Lazzaroni di Saronno brand, packed in elegant red tins. There is also a sweet liqueur called *amaretto,* made from almonds.

ANCHOVIES: One of the so-called blue fish (others are garfish and sardines) that are common in Italian seas all year round. Like Mediterranean sardines, anchovies are rather small. They are usually preserved whole in salt, and are thoroughly washed and boned and the heads removed before use. Already cleaned fillets preserved in oil are often used. In Liguria raw anchovies are used, "cooked" only in lemon juice.

ARBORIO RICE: A plump, oval-shaped grain, shorter and rounder than the American short-grain rice. The best-quality Arborio rice grows in the Po Valley region of Piedmont. It is used in sweet and savory dishes and is at its finest when cooked in *risotto.*

BATTUTO: Literally, "beaten"; in cooking terminology this refers to a mixture of finely chopped herbs, celery, onion and carrots.

BEET (BEETROOT): A much-used vegetable that requires lengthy cooking, generally in the oven. It can be bought precooked in almost any greengrocer's shop. Nowadays beets are cooked commercially and are sold canned or in airtight packs.

BIGOLI: A larger form of spaghetti, homemade using only water, flour and a small amount of egg. They are a specialty of the Veneto and are served with a duck sauce.

BISCOTTI DI PRATO (also known as *cantucci* or *cantuccini*): Hard-textured sweet cookies with almond pieces, which keep for long periods and are now exported all over the world. They can be rather dry, and are often eaten dipped in *vin santo.*

BOLLITO: Literally, "boiled"; a method of cooking widely used for meat. A *bollito* is generally made up of different kinds of meat such as beef, veal, tongue, chicken and the spiced pork sausage known as *cotechino.* It is served with a green parsley sauce. To make a good *bollito,* the meat must be put into water that is already boiling.

BOMBA DI RISO: A molded rice dish with a rich filling of ground meat cooked with various flavorings: herbs, mushrooms, diced cheese, ham, etc. The "rice bombe" is a specialty of the Parma area, and a similar dish made in Naples is called *sartù di riso.*

BRASATO: Literally, "braised"; a method of cooking over low heat with just a little liquid. At one time it was done in a pan with embers placed on the lid (the word charcoal or embers is *brace,* hence *brasare,* to braise). Today this kind of cooking is done in the oven. A *brasato* is also sometimes known as a *stufato.*

BRODETTO: The name given to the fish soup of the Adriatic area. In Livorno it is called *caciucco,* in other regions simply *zuppa di pesce* (fish soup).

BRODO: Italian cooks make a broth or stock that is very light, using only chicken, beef, veal or fish without bones, and vegetables. They never use cooked bones as the French do. Sometimes uncooked bones are added if a jellied stock is desired, together with a trotter or snout.

BRUSCHETTA: Generally served before a meal, a very popular dish made with coarse-textured bread, toasted over coals and liberally dressed with extra virgin olive oil. In Tuscany it is called *fett'unta* or *fregolotta.*

BUTTER: In Italy, butter is never salted.

CACIOCAVALLO: A hard white cheese with a light rind that keeps well. It is a bulk cheese with a rather strong taste, made from cow's milk.

CALAMARI: Squid (*calamaretti* if they are small); *seppie* are cuttlefish.

CARBONARA: *Spaghetti alla carbonara* is so named because in times gone by it was the usual fare for woodsmen to take as their lunch when they went to make charcoal *(carbone)*. It is a complete meal on its own, containing *pancetta* and eggs.

CARPACCIO: A cold dish of raw meat that is sliced paper-thin and usually dressed with oil and lemon juice. Various seasonings may be added, such as flakes of Parmesan, chopped lemon rind or parsley. It was named after the famous Venetian painter by the proprietor of Harry's Bar in Venice, but its origin is definitely Piedmontese.

CAUL FAT: A very thin membrane with veins of white fat, which covers the internal organs of the pig. It must always be soaked in warm water before use to soften. Thin slices of fatty bacon can be substituted.

CIMA RIPIENA: A Genoese dish made of veal breast with a pocket cut into it, which is stuffed with one of various fillings.

CODA DI MANZO (OXTAIL): Especially popular in Latium, where it is served stewed and used in soups and *minestroni*. It has excellent flavor but requires a long cooking time.

COOKING UTENSILS: In Italian a number of different terms are used to describe the same thing. More important than the terminology is the material: different types are suitable for different methods of cooking.

Tegame is the term used for the round wide shallow pan, usually of terracotta, which is used for cooking sauces, braising meats and stewing vegetables. Terracotta pans diffuse the heat particularly well.

Padella is a skillet, usually of cast iron, which is used above all for deep frying and for sautéing sliced meat and vegetables.

Teglia is a round, wide, shallow pan of copper, aluminum or stainless steel. It has two handles and is suitable for braising or roasting meat and vegetables.

Casseruola is a saucepan with higher sides. Italians cook in heavy aluminum when the objective is for the food (usually meat) to stick to the bottom of the pan, so that browned bits can then be scraped up by stirring in stock or wine at the end of cooking to form a sauce or gravy. Stainless steel is used for *risotto*, soups, stocks and tomato sauce and for boiling pasta, meat or fish.

A cast iron skillet is used for frying such dishes as *fritto misto*, fried potatoes (chips), etc.

Terracotta saucepans are used for tomato and meat sauces.

Tinned copper is the material used for cooking polenta and for baked dishes like lasagne and *cannelloni*.

Ceramic dishes are also used in the oven—not for meat because the juices are better retained in aluminum dishes, but for lasagne, *cannelloni* and gratinéed vegetables.

COSTOLETTE (CUTLETS): Rather thick slices of meat cut from the bony part, particularly the ribs (hence the name *costolette*, from *costole*, ribs). The meat close to the bone is always tastier and tenderer. Cutlets are normally cooked in butter or oil after they have been dipped in egg and coated with breadcrumbs.

CREAM: There is only one kind of cream in Italy. It is not a thickened cream and is always used fresh.

CREMA DI VERDURA: Purée of vegetables, often with cream or milk added. Sometimes it is thickened with puréed potatoes or sieved cooked rice.

CRESCENZA: A very delicate, creamy cheese typical of Lombardy. It is also sometimes known as *robiola*, the best-known brand being Introbio. When aged, it takes on a very strong flavor and develops a crust.

CROSTINI: One of the most common types of *antipasto* in Italian cooking. Among the best known of the hundreds of varieties are the Tuscan *crostini di milza* (croutons with spleen).

DRIED MUSHROOMS: Always means dried *porcini* (boletus) mushrooms, which grow in chestnut or oak woods after the rains, while the weather is still warm.

DRIED PASTA: There is an almost infinite variety of dried pasta in Italy, known by an equally large number of names according to region. Spaghetti is the most popular type, and it is cooked in a few minutes in a large amount of water with added salt but no oil.

It must be quite firm to the bite *(al dente)*, and as soon as it is drained the prepared sauce should be mixed into it.

EGGS: A caution on eggs. In recent years there has been increased concern about the threat of contracting salmonellosis (a food-borne illness caused by salmonella bacteria) from raw or lightly cooked eggs. Some recipes in this book are made with the above. The amount of risk is very slight, but it should be noted that those who are elderly, very young or immunocompromised will be the most seriously affected if stricken with food poisoning. An egg mixture that is heated to 165°F (75°C) is safe.

FENNEL: A sweet, anis-flavored white bulb that is eaten raw in salads. The male plant, with its rounder bulb, is preferred for salads; the more elongated female bulb is usually cooked. For fennel to be white, it must be continuously covered with earth as the plant grows.

FINOCCHIONA: A Tuscan salami that contains fennel *(finocchio)* seeds. In contrast to most salamis, it must never be allowed to age.

FONDUE: A Piedmontese dish based on melted fontina cheese, from which it gets its name, *fonduta* (in Piedmontese *fondua*), meaning "melted." *Fonduta* is also used as a sauce for *risotto,* added at the end of cooking, and in a very elegant dish consisting of a large vol-au-vent filled with *agnolotti*, over which the fondue is poured. When served with truffles it is usually presented in individual ramekins.

FONTANA (FOUNTAIN): The instructions for making pasta in Italian usually begin with: *"Mettere la farina a fontana sulla tavola . . ."* (literally, put the flour in the shape of a fountain on the table). The tip of the "fountain" is then widened to form a well into which the eggs or liquid required to form the dough are placed.

FRITTATA: The most common form of *frittata* in Italy is the one resembling a flattened cake of eggs, possibly with other ingredients such as vegetables, cheese or fish. The rolled variety, more common in France, is called *omeletta.* Both the *frittata* and the *omeletta* are always cooked in a heavy cast iron or nonstick skillet, never in the oven. This type of mixture cooked in the oven becomes a *tortino,* which is drier in the center. A good Italian *frittata* must be *bavosa*—liquid in the center.

FRITTO MISTO ("MIXED FRY"): One of the most typical Italian dishes, which may be interpreted in many ways according to region. In Piedmont it is very rich, with little fruit fritters or semolina pancakes as well as different kinds of meat fried in butter. In Tuscany it consists basically of white meats, in Latium of lamb and artichokes or brains; in the south it is based on fish such as young squid or rings of cuttlefish; and sometimes cubes of smoked mozzarella are included.

GAMBERETTI AND *SCAMPI:* Both refer to shrimp (prawns).

GINESTRATA: A traditional light and very nutritious soup, which in the old days was seen as nourishing food for the elderly and for young children.

GNOCCHI: The name for small balls of potato, spinach or other ingredients. The name is also given to discs of semolina in Rome, and of polenta in the Veneto.

GORGONZOLA: A full-fat cheese with green mold veins, a specialty of a small town of the same name near Milan. Both mild and strong varieties are available.

GUANCIALE: Pig's cheek, a much sought-after delicacy that is cured with salt and pepper in the same way as *pancetta.* It is, however, rarer and more choice than *pancetta.*

IMPANATO (FROM *PANE,* BREAD): The word used to describe meat, vegetables or fish that have first been dipped into beaten egg, then coated in breadcrumbs and cooked.

INSALATA VERDE: Green salad, usually meaning lettuce. Sometimes a green salad may also be made with curly endive or other varieties of lettuce known as *scarola* (escarole) and *valerianella* (lamb's lettuce). They are rarely mixed, only one type being served at a time. The salad is normally dressed only with extra virgin olive oil, vinegar and salt.

LASAGNE: Squares of fresh or dried pasta that are boiled in water, then drained and layered with various sauces. Among the most famous ways of serving lasagne are *alla bolognese,* with meat and mushroom sauce, and *al pesto,* with Ligurian basil sauce.

LEPRE: Hare, which is hung in its skin for several days before cooking. Wild rabbit, whose flesh has a slightly more delicate flavor, is prepared in the same way as hare.

MACCHERONI ALLA CHITARRA: The *chitarra* is a traditional kitchen utensil shaped like a guitar, with sharp cutting wires on which the sheets of pasta are laid so that when a rolling pin is passed over them, the pasta is cut into thin strips.

MALFATTI: Gnocchi of spinach and ricotta; a specialty of Tuscany, where they are also sometimes called *ravioli nudi* (naked ravioli) because they have no pasta covering.

MARROW: The internal part of the shank (shin) bone in beef or veal, used in cooking various dishes. The classic example is the Milanese *risotto,* which is cooked in equal parts of melted butter and marrow. The marrow gives the rice a special creamy consistency and it is also less fatty than butter. It is very easy to extract from the bone with finger pressure. Sometimes it is boiled before use. The marrow from the bones in *ossi buchi in gremolata* (recipe page 62) is particularly good.

MARSALA: A sweet dessert wine from the area around the city of Marsala in Sicily. It is widely used in Italian cooking for meat, vegetable and sweet dishes. The Venetian dessert *zabaglione al marsala* is famous; the wine was familiar to the Venetians from very early times, because they were able to travel the length of the country in their ships as far back as the era of the Crusades.

MELON: Italian melons are generally round, with a slightly lined skin and a pale orange color. They are very fragrant and are only to be found in late summer. Melon is often served with prosciutto as a first course, although prosciutto is equally tasty served with figs.

MINESTRA: A thin soup with chopped vegetables, often with rice or the special small pasta made for soups. *Minestra* may also be chicken or vegetable broth in which these small pasta shapes *(pastina)* are cooked.

MINESTRONE: A vegetable soup with rice or pasta, in which the vegetables are cut into larger pieces than those for *minestra.* The soup usually contains dried legumes such as white beans, lentils or chickpeas.

MOSTARDA DI CREMONA: Cremona mustard, a specialty of the city of Cremona, made from candied fruit preserved in a sweet syrup lightly spiced with mustard. It is an excellent accompaniment for boiled meat.

MOZZARELLA: A rindless white cheese made from buffalo milk, which is much sought after and becoming increasingly difficult to find. The only areas producing it are Salerno and Caserta. Mozzarella is now also commercially produced using cow's milk, but it has much less flavor.

MUSSELS: Known as *cozze* in many areas, and in others as *muscoli* or *pecei.* A similar mollusk is called *dattero di mare,* or date mussel. Highly prized and having an elongated light brown shell, it is found in the area around La Spezia.

OIL: In general, extra virgin olive oil is used. It contains less than 1% acidity and should be cold pressed. Not only does it have no cholesterol, it apparently actually helps to dissolve cholesterol.

OLIVES: The best are those in brine (a mixture of water and salt) or preserved in oil. Less delicate in taste are the olives preserved in vinegar. The black ones have the strongest flavor. In general, Italian olives are rather small.

ORECCHIETTE ("LITTLE EARS"): A slightly concave pasta made by forming little balls of dough with the hands and pressing a hollow into the center of each. Today it may be bought in shops. It has quite a long cooking time and is often served with a lamb or other meat sauce, or simply with tomato sauce.

OVOLI: A highly prized mushroom that resembles an egg and has a bright orange cap. It is generally eaten raw as a salad.

PAGLIA E FIENO ("STRAW AND HAY"): *Taglierini* that are half green, made with spinach, and half white, using only egg. They are served simply with melted butter and Parmesan cheese, or with reduced cream and Parmesan.

PAN DI NATALE ("CHRISTMAS BREAD"): A term used to cover many traditional Christmas cakes of varying shapes and textures. The basis is generally a soft, sweet yeast dough, to which candied fruit, raisins, pine nuts, etc. are added. One of the classic versions is the Genoese *pan dolce.*

Pan Pepato: A cake characteristic of Umbria. It is made with nuts, raisins, almonds, chocolate and hazelnuts and flavored with nutmeg and pepper.

Pan di Spagna: A light-textured cake in which only eggs, flour and a little butter are used. It serves as a base for many Italian desserts, generally being soaked in some kind of liqueur and combined with whipped cream and perhaps cooked fruit. It forms the basis of the dessert known as *zuppa inglese* (which is something like a trifle).

Pancetta: Unsmoked bacon from the belly of the pig; it may be flat or rolled. It is cured with spices, salt and pepper.

Pandoro: A cake traditionally served at Christmastime in the city of Verona, but now also produced commercially year-round. It is very light in texture, like a sponge cake, and is shaped like an octagonal cone.

Panettone: The classic Milanese cake, now made commercially and sold all over the world. Usually shaped as a tall round loaf, it consists of a sweet yeast dough with candied fruits and raisins. It is a difficult cake to make at home, tending to be rather heavy.

Panforte: Typical of the city of Siena, now also made commercially and exported throughout the world. It is a flat, very rich cake containing walnuts, almonds, hazelnuts, honey, candied fruits and lots of spices. It is said to have been carried by the Crusaders on their expeditions because of its energy-giving properties.

Pangrattato or *Pane Grattugiato* ("grated bread"): Breadcrumbs produced by drying out stale bread in the oven and processing it in a food processor until it is like coarse sand. The name derives from the fact that the bread used to be grated to produce the crumbs. Breadcrumbs are now sold in transparent packs and also exported.

Panzanella: Stale bread salad, typical of Tuscany. In times past, Tuscan bread was baked once a week, without salt (as it still is today), because salt was very costly and indeed was used as a means of exchange. It is worth noting that salt-free bread stays fresh longer. There are also well-known soups based on stale bread: *pappa al pomodoro,* also a Tuscan specialty; the

Milanese *pancotto;* and the *acquacotta* of Grosseto, in which an egg is added to each serving.

Parmesan: A hard cheese with a thick crust that is aged for at least two years. It is a specialty of Parma and Reggio-Emilia and the one with *parmigiano reggiano* branded on the crust is the best. It is served freshly grated over many dishes.

Pecorino: A cheese made from ewe's milk that is popular in various regions. In Tuscany it is fairly mild and may be sold fresh or aged. In Sardinia it is usually saltier and stronger in flavor.

Pesto: A sauce obtained by pounding basil, garlic, oil and pine nuts in a mortar. It is a specialty of the city of Genoa.

Piadina: A soft type of flat bread made in Emilia-Romagna, usually eaten with salami or prosciutto. It may also be filled with sautéed spinach or ricotta.

Pinzimonio: A way of presenting raw vegetables that involves dipping them in bowls filled with extra virgin olive oil, salt and pepper. The Piedmontese version of *pinzimonio* is the *bagna cauda,* a cooked sauce made up of half butter and half olive oil, with a few fillets of anchovy and some chopped garlic blended in. This sauce is kept simmering in a terracotta saucepan in the center of the table, and the diners dip their *crudités* into it.

Pizza: The same shape as the *schiacciata* and made from the same dough. The difference is that the seasoning used on pizza is far richer and contains a number of different elements such as vegetables, mozzarella or other types of cheese, prosciutto, etc. It is considered to be a first course, in contrast to the *schiacciata,* which is seen as bread enriched with added flavor.

Pizzaiola: A style of cooking that uses the basic ingredients of pizza topping: oil, tomato and oregano. Steak, leftover boiled meat, or fish may be served *alla pizzaiola.*

Pizzelle: Deep-fried pizza dough, popular in many areas of Italy and used in different ways. It may be eaten plain or with tomato sauce, sautéed vegetables or cheese.

POLENTA: A typical Venetian dish made from coarse-ground cornmeal that is sprinkled into boiling water and stirred as it cooks. It must be fairly firm when cooked and is often served simply with fried sage leaves, melted butter and grated Parmesan. Or it may be sliced and seasoned in any number of ways—with meat or fish sauces, sausages, mushrooms, cheese, etc. Normally it is made with yellow cornmeal, but sometimes the Venetians use more finely ground white cornmeal.

PROSCIUTTO: Ham from the pig's hind leg, one of the most common foods in the Italian diet. It may be raw (crudo) or cooked (cotto). Though usually unsmoked, in Alto Adige and Trentino it is also sold smoked.

PUNTARELLE: A special Roman salad green, served only in winter. The stalks, which are very long with a needle-like serrated leaf, curl when cut. This salad is served with a dressing consisting of oil, vinegar, salt, an anchovy fillet in oil, and crushed garlic.

RADICCHIO ROSSO (RED CHICORY): Various types are available, the most sought after being the radicchio di Treviso, which is whitened in the cellar under sand or compost before being sold. It has elongated leaves with long, soft white ribs and a dark red color just at the tips of the leaves. The most common radicchi are those from Castelfranco Veneto (small and round like a ball, with wrinkly leaves and a rather bitter taste) and Chioggia (very similar, but a lighter red in color).

RIBOLLITA: A famous Tuscan bean soup made with black cabbage, a dark-colored vegetable with elongated leaves. Like all other types of cabbage, this one is at its best after the first night frosts, because it becomes softer and more flavorful.

RICCIARELLI: Sienese almond cookies (biscuits).

RICOTTA ("RECOOKED"): A very light cheese made from milk that has been cooked twice. Traditional ricotta is made from pure ewe's milk; it is still found in Tuscany, Latium and Sardinia. A far less tasty ricotta made from cow's milk is to be found in other Italian regions.

RISOTTO: Rice cooked in broth (stock) that is added gradually so the rice remains just covered throughout cooking. The most suitable type of rice is Arborio,

with its large, oval-shaped grain. When cooked, risotto must be al dente (still firm to the bite) and have the consistency of porridge. It normally cooks in about 16 minutes. From the time the broth is added, a risotto must be stirred constantly, and it is not possible to stop the cooking and finish it off at a later time.

SAFFRON: The stamens of the crocus, a flower that grows around l'Aquila in the Abruzzi region and is also cultivated there specifically for saffron. Kashmir is another major exporter of saffron. Crocuses need rather cold winters and hot summers for their development. The most expensive saffron is sold in the form of dried whole stamens; the less valuable powdered kind is more generally available.

SALSICCIA: Italian sausage goes by various names. In Lombardy and the Veneto, for example, it is called luganega. In northern and central Italy, as a general rule sausage is not spicy; ground pork is simply seasoned with salt and pepper and then put into the sausage skin. In the south, sausage is very hot. It may be thick or thin, long without links tied off, or fatter and divided into short lengths. The sausages of Tuscany are famous, particularly those produced in the Chianti area. They are fried and presented on a bed of beans cooked with tomato, oil, garlic and abundant fresh sage.

SALTIMBOCCA: Literally, "jump into the mouth," so tasty is this veal dish. Sometimes the slices of veal are rolled around the filling, and in this case they may go by various names—messicani, rollatini, bauletti (suitcases), involtini—and have any number of fillings, from rich to very simple.

SAOR: A method of cooking food in a sweet and sour sauce containing vinegar. It is very common in several Italian regions, especially in the Veneto and the south. In Tuscany the saor is called agrodolce (sharp and sweet) or dolceforte (sweet and strong). The dolceforte method is particularly suited to cooking boar; it is made with melted bitter chocolate and raisins.

SCAMORZA: A white cheese made with whole cow's milk, pear-shaped and with a smooth, thin rind.

SCHIACCIATA: The Tuscan name for a particular kind of bread, rolled out thinly like a pizza and seasoned only with oil and salt. Sometimes it is enriched with rosemary or sage. In Liguria the same bread is known as *focaccia.* Sometimes sliced onions or small pieces of olives are used instead of herbs.

SCOTTADITO ("BURNING FINGER"): Small cutlets on the bone, which are eaten with the fingers. They are eaten very hot, hence their name.

SOFFRITTO: A mixture of chopped vegetables (usually carrots, onions, celery and parsley, but it varies from region to region) fried in oil or butter, used to flavor soups, sauces and meat dishes.

SOPA COADA: A famous soup from the Veneto that consists of layers of bread alternated with layers of boned roast pigeon. The name derives from the fact that it requires a very long cooking time (*sopa* is a regional word for soup; *coada* comes from *covare,* to hatch).

SPAGHETTI: Factory-produced dried pasta strings made with flour and water. There are various forms of dried pasta with many different names: *penne, penne rigate, bucatini, farfalle, fusilli, rigatoni,* etc. Dried pasta, found particularly in the south, takes oil-based sauces, often with tomato, vegetables or fish.

SPELT: A kind of hard wheat with the husk, which must be soaked in water before use. It was popular with the ancient Romans and is now widely used in Umbria and Latium and throughout the Middle East. It is used as the main ingredient for soups, both thick and thin.

STRACOTTO: Another word for *brasato* or *stufato,* braised or stewed meat. *Stracotto* is the name used specifically for a Piedmontese meat dish cooked in this way, and it means, literally, "overcooked."

STRUTTO: Melted pork fat, which in some regions is known as *sugna* (lard). Foods fried in it are especially light and crisp.

SWISS CHARD: The white stalks of Swiss chard are served in many ways—with a sauce, with butter and cheese, boiled and dressed with oil, etc.

TAGLIATELLE: Handmade pasta cut just 3/8 in (1 cm) wide and a millimeter thick, a specialty of northern and central Italy. In some regions it is called *fettuccine* or *taglierini.* The Tuscan variety, *pappardelle,* is cut into strips more than double the width of *tagliatelle.* The pasta is made with flour and eggs and served with butter-based sauces.

TIMBALLO: *Timbale* is the name usually given to pasta that is cooked in a mold and filled with meat or vegetables. *Timballo di maccheroni* with a sweet crust is a specialty of the Campania region.

TORRONE: A sweet nougat based on honey and almonds, a specialty of the Cremona area. In other areas *torrone* may also contain figs or chocolate.

TROFIE: A kind of handmade pasta shaped like slightly elongated gnocchi. It is a specialty of the town of Camogli in Liguria, and is usually served with pesto sauce.

TRUFFLES *(TARTUFI)*: Found near the roots of oak or chestnut trees during October, November and December. They grow fairly deep below the surface and dogs are specially trained to identify their scent. Before a truffle is completely exposed, the dog is removed and man takes over so that there is no risk of damaging the truffle.

The most precious are the very light-colored truffles that grow in Alba, in the Piedmont region. Less tasty ones are also found in some parts of the Marches and Tuscany. Black truffles are common in Umbria, but they are less flavorful and not so precious. The truffles from Alba can be priced as high as 300,000 lire for 100 grams.

VIN SANTO: A Tuscan dessert wine made from grapes that have been dried away from direct sunlight for a couple of months before pressing. The wine is aged for four or five years, sealed in small oak casks kept under the rooftops so that it is exposed to temperature variations.

ZUCCHINI FLOWERS: Plentiful in Italy when zucchini begin to grow. Usually the male flower—not the female, which goes on to produce the vegetable—is used for cooking. The male flower is recognized by its thinner stem. The zucchini flowers must be picked and eaten while they are still firmly closed.

ZUPPA: A soup, usually vegetable, meat or fish, that is poured over fried or oven-toasted bread.

INDEX

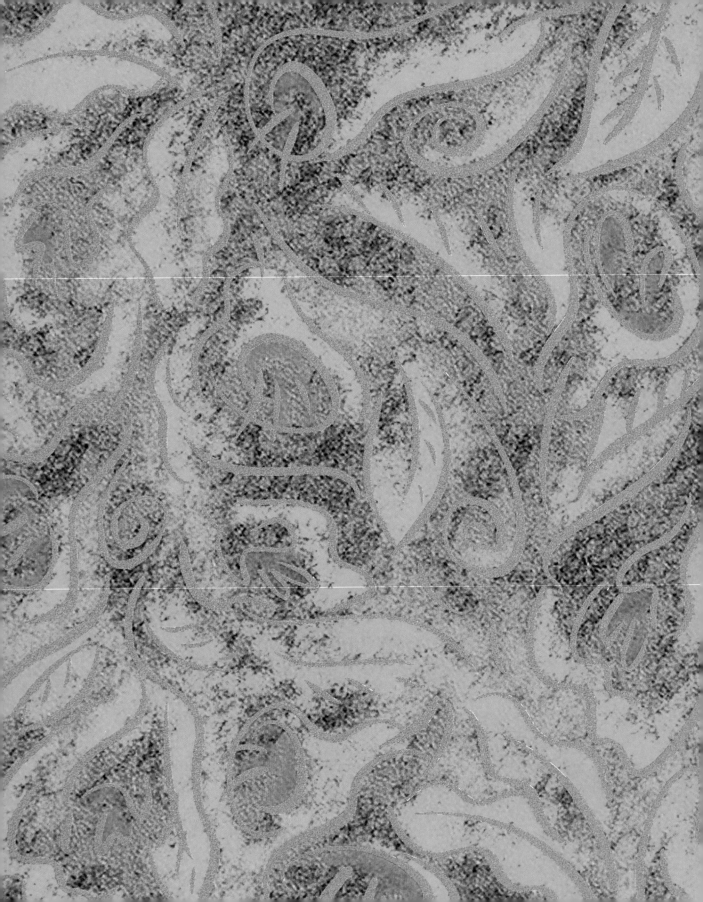